EDEXCEL GCSE 9-1
Maths Higher
Practice Exam Papers

Gordon Goulding

i

Contents

General Certificate of Secondary Education

Name _____

Surname _____

EDEXCEL GCSE Mathematics

Candidate Number

Centre Number

SET A Paper 1 (Non-Calculator)

Higher Tier
Time allowed: 1 hour 30 minutes

Total marks: 80

Materials
You may use a ruler, eraser, compass, protractor, pen, pencil and tracing paper.

Instructions
- Answer all the questions.
- Answer the question on the spaces provided.
- Use of calculators is not allowed.

Information
- The marks are shown for each question in the bracket.
- Method marks are given even if your answer is incorrect.
- Unless otherwise noted, diagrams are not drawn to scale.

Recommendations
- Read each question carefully.
- Check your answers thoroughly.

Answer ALL questions.
Write your answers in the spaces provided.
Show all the steps of your calculation.

1   Work out the value of $\dfrac{2^4 \times 2}{2^8 \times 2^0}$.

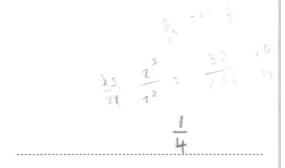

$\dfrac{1}{4}$

(Total for question 1 is 1 mark)

2

(a) Make x the subject of $y = mx + c$

$\dfrac{y-c}{m} = x$

(1)

Given that $y = 10, c = -4, m = -2$ and $y = mx + c$

(b) Work out the value of x.

$\dfrac{10 - -4}{-2} \quad \dfrac{6}{-2}$

$10 = -2x$ ⁶⁄₋₂ ₌ ₃

-3

(1)

(Total for question 2 is 2 marks)

3

Describe fully the single transformation that maps triangle **P** into **Q**.

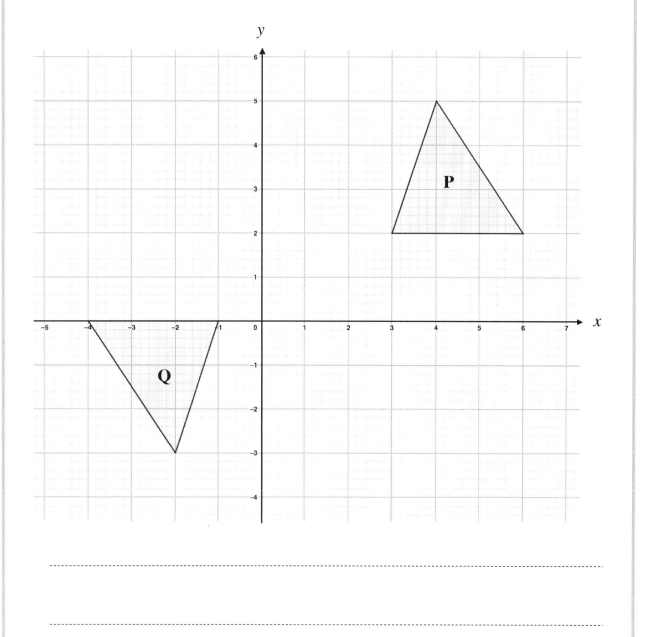

....

....

(2)

(Total for question 3 is 2 marks)

4

Joe and Mark's monthly salaries are in the ratio of 4 : 3.
Mark and Annic's monthly salary are in the ratio 5 : 8.

(a) What is the ratio of Joe's salary to Annie's salary? Give your answer in its simplest form

----

(2)

Joe earns £2000 each month.

(b) How much do Mark and Annie earn individually? Who has the highest monthly salary ?
You must show how you get your answers.

Annie £ ---

Mark £ ---

highest salary earned by: ---

(3)

(Total for question 4 is 5 marks)

5

The diagram shows a rectangle with length 8 *cm* and width of 4 *cm*.
AM is an arc of the circle with centre *D*.

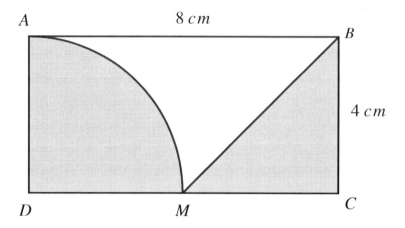

Show that:

$$\frac{\text{Area of unshaded region}}{\text{Area of sector } ADM} = \frac{6-\pi}{\pi}$$

(Total for question 5 is 4 marks)

6

(a) Write down the exact value of cos(30)

----

(1)

Here is the right-angled triangle ABC

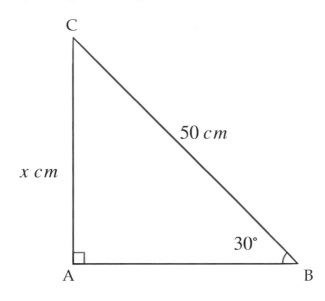

(b) Work out the value of x

----

(2)

(Total for question 6 is 3 marks)

7

(a) Simplify fully $\dfrac{(x+1)(x+2)}{2(x+1)^2}$.

----

(1)

(b) Factorise fully $162 - 2k^2$.

----

(2)

(Total for question 7 is 3 marks)

The table shows information about the weights of tomatoes Joe harvested this year.

Highest value	158g
Median	118g
Interquartile range	50g
Lowest value	51g
Lower quartile	84g

(a) Draw a box plot to represent this information in the grid below.

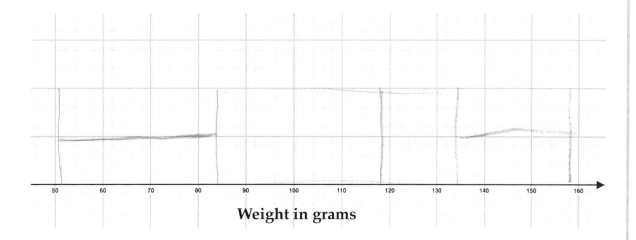

Weight in grams

(3)

The box plot below shows the distribution of weight of his tomatoes from last year.

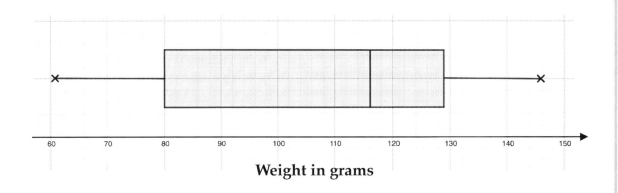

Weight in grams

(b) Compare the distribution of the weights of his last year's tomatoes with the distribution of the weights of tomatoes this year.

----

(2)

(Total for question 8 is 5 marks)

9

It would take 3 taps 4 hours to fill 5 water tanks.

(*a*) How many minutes will it take to fill 5 water tanks if only 2 taps were used ?

$$3 \quad \quad \times \frac{4}{1} = \frac{6}{3}$$

$$\frac{480}{3} = 160$$

_____ 160 _____ minutes

(2)

(*b*) State one assumption you made in working out your answer to part (*a*).

_____

_____ The taps all work at the same speed _____

(1)

(*c*) How many taps are required to fill 8 tanks in **under** 6 hours ?

_____ Taps

(3)

(Total for question 9 is 6 marks)

10

Prove algebraically that $1.\dot{4}$ can be written as $\frac{13}{9}$.

$1.\dot{4} = x$

$14.\dot{4} = 10x$

$14.\dot{4} - 1.\dot{4} = 13 = 9x$

$x = 1.\dot{4} = \frac{13}{9}$

11

(a) Work out the value of $\left(\dfrac{343}{64}\right)^{-\frac{2}{3}}$.

$$\sqrt{\dfrac{343^{3}}{64}} \quad \dfrac{64}{343} = \dfrac{\cancel{8}^{4}}{77} \approx \dfrac{16}{\cancel{49}}$$

$$\dfrac{16}{49}$$

(2)

(b)

If $7\sqrt{7} = 7^{x}$ $\quad \dfrac{1}{7\sqrt{7}} = 7^{y-2}$,

Work out the value of $\dfrac{x \times y}{3}$.

(3)

(Total for question 11 is 5 marks)

12

Show that $\dfrac{\left(\sqrt{12}-\sqrt{3}\right)^2}{\sqrt{3}+1}$ can be written in the form $a + b\sqrt{3}$ where a, b are rational numbers.

(Total for question 12 is 3 marks)

13

These three spheres are mathematically similar .

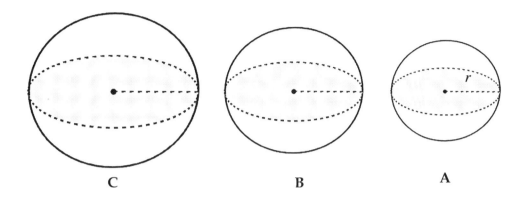

C   B   A

Surface area of sphere **A** is $16\pi\ cm^2$.
Surface area of sphere **B** is $36\pi\ cm^2$.
The ratio of the radius of sphere **B** to the sphere **C** is 3 : 4
Show that the ratio of volume of shape **A** to the volume of shape **C** is
1 : 8.

(Total for question 13 is 3 marks)

14

Given that
$$f(x) = (2x - 1)^2, \quad g(x) = x - 1$$

(a) Show that $fg(x) = ax^2 + bx + c$ where a, b, c are constants.

a -----------------------------

b -----------------------------

c -----------------------------

(b) Find x when $fg(x) = 9$

(3)

----

(2)

(Total for question 14 is 5 marks)

15

Graph crosses the x axis at -2 and 6.
y intercept of the graph is at -1.
Equation of the curve is $y = ax^2 + bx + c$.

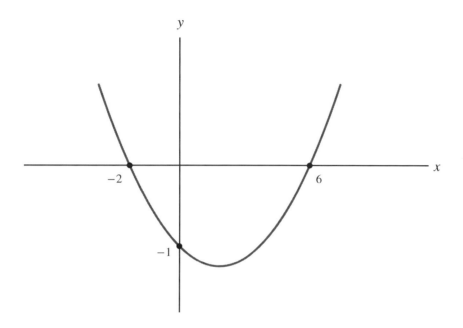

Find the value of constants a, b and c.

a ----------------------------------

b ----------------------------------

c ----------------------------------

(Total for question 15 is 4 marks)

16

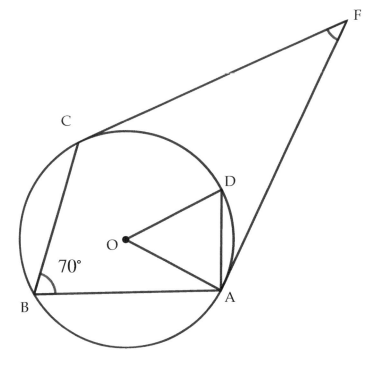

A, B, C, D are points on the circumference of the circle with centre O. CF and AF are tangent to the circle at C and A respectively.

$A\hat{B}C = 70°$

Work out the size of the angle $C\hat{F}A$.

Give a reason for each stage of your answer.

----

(4)

(Total for question 16 is 4 marks)

17

The graphs of $y = f(x)$ is shown below.
(a) Sketch the graph of $y = f(x) - 2$ on the same grid below.

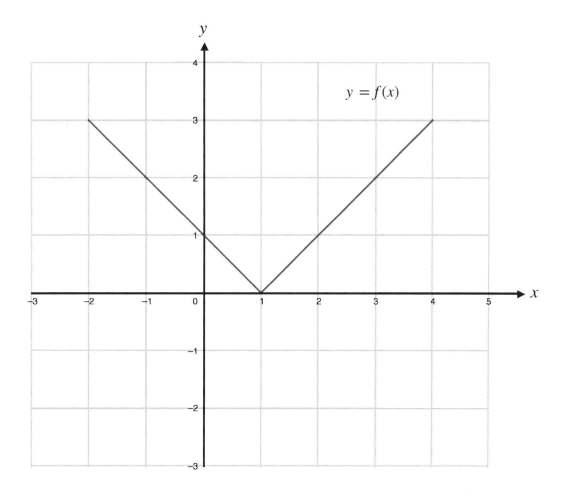

(2)

17

Graph $y = h(x)$ is translated to give graph **A**.

(b) Write down the equation of graph **A** in terms of $h(x)$

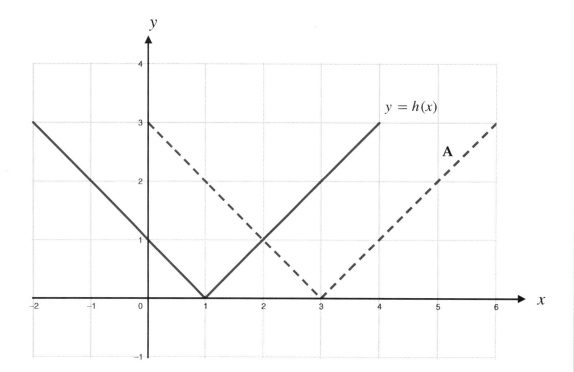

(1)

(Total for question 17 is 3 marks)

18

x is an integer such that

$x^2 < 16$ and $\dfrac{8-x}{2} < x + 1$.

Find the value of x.

----

(5)

(Total for question 18 is 5 marks)

19

y is directly proportional to u.

u is directly proportional to the square root of x.

When $y = 8$, $u = 4$

When $u = 2$, $x = 9$

Find the value of y when the value of x is 36.

(4)

(Total for question 19 is 4 marks)

20

Triangle AOB and triangle MAN are mathematically similar.
M and N are on the line OA and AB, respectively.

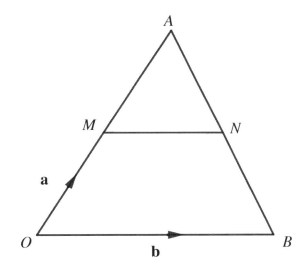

$\overrightarrow{OM} : \overrightarrow{MA}$ is $2 : 1$
$\overrightarrow{OA} = \mathbf{a}$ and $\overrightarrow{OB} = \mathbf{b}$
Work out $\overrightarrow{ON}$.

(Total for question 20 is 4 marks)

21

There are only red and blue balls in the box. The ratio of red to blue balls is 2 : 3.

Ali takes a ball from the bag at random.

Tina then takes another ball from the bag at random.

The probability that they both take out the same colour balls is $\frac{1}{2}$.

Work out the number of balls of each colour in the box.

Red balls   ------------------------------------

Blue balls   ------------------------------

(Total for question 21 is 6 marks)

End of the paper

Name _____

Surname_____

EDEXCEL GCSE Mathematics

Candidate Number

Centre Number

SET A Paper 2 (Calculator)

Higher Tier
Time allowed: 1 hour 30 minutes

Total marks: 80

Materials
You may use a ruler, eraser, compass, protractor, pen, pencil and tracing paper.

Instructions
- Answer all the questions.
- Answer the question on the spaces provided.
- Use of calculators is allowed.

Information
- The marks are shown for each question in the bracket.
- Method marks are given even if your answer is incorrect.
- Unless otherwise noted, diagrams are not drawn to scale.

Recommendations
- Read each question carefully.
- Check your answers thoroughly.

Answer ALL the questions.
Write your answers in the spaces provided.
Show all the steps of your calculation.

1

$a = 3.1, \quad b = -2.123, \quad c = 6.2$

(a) Calculate the value of $\sqrt{\dfrac{a+b}{c}}$.

Write down all the figures on your calculator display.

----

(1)

(b) Round your answer to part (a) to two significant figures.

----

(1)

(Total for question 1 is 2 marks)

2

Last year Jessica bought her sandals for £35. This year she pays £43.5 for the same pair of sandals.
Work out the percentage increase in the cost of her sandals.
Give your answer correct to two decimal places.

%
----

(2)

(Total for question 2 is 2 marks)

3

(a) Complete the table of values for $y = 3 - x - x^2$

x	-4	-3	-2	-1	0	1	2
y	-9				3		-3

(b) Draw the graph of $y = 3 - x - x^2$ on the axes below.　　　　(2)

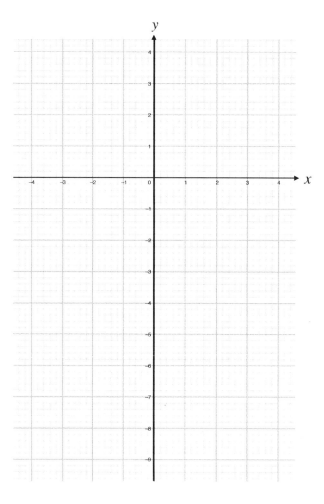

(2)

(c) Use the graph to estimate the co-ordinate of the turning point.

----

(1)

(Total for question 3 is 5 marks)

4

Arnav can complete a 1600m race in 4 minutes 32 seconds.

(a) Assuming his speed is the same for each race, work out how long he takes to complete a1km race. Give your answer in minutes and seconds.

----

(3)

Arnav's average speed actually increases when he participates in a shorter race.

(b) How does this affect your answer to part (a)?

----

(1)

(Total for question 4 is 4 marks)

5

ξ = {numbers between 1 and 12}

A = {prime numbers between 1 and 12}

B = {even numbers between 1 and 12 }

C = {odd numbers between 1 and 12}

(a) Complete the Venn diagram using the information.

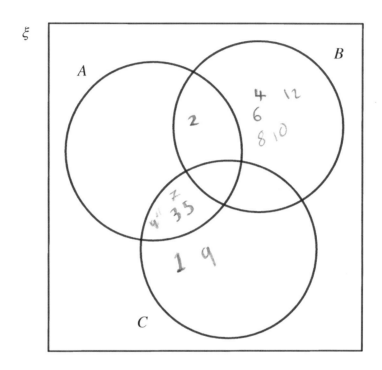

(3)

(b) Find the probability of $p(A \cap B')$

(1)

(Total for question 5 is 4 marks)

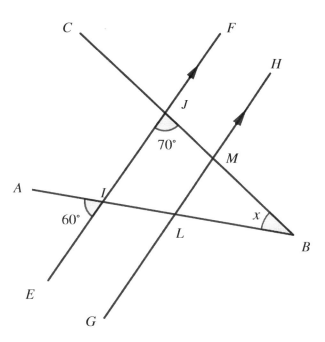

In this diagram EF and GH are parallel lines that intersect lines CB and AB at the vertex I, J, M and L as shown.

Angle $AIE = 60°$

Angle $IJM = 70°$

Work out the value of x.

Give reasons for each stages of your working.

(Total for question 6 is 3 marks)

This diagram shows a design dimension of Tom's living room floor.

The floor is made up of a rectangle and four semi-circles.

He is going to paint the floor. Each 4*l* tin of paint costs £24.50. One litre of paint covers $2.4m^2$

Tom has budgeted £80 to spend on paint.

Has Tom got enough money to buy all the paint he needs?

You must show all your work.

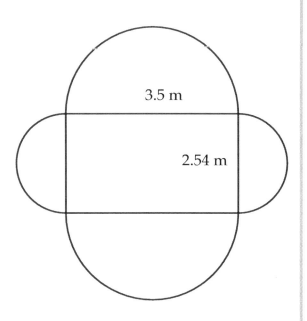

3.5 m

2.54 m

(Total for question 7 is 6 marks)

Timothy wants to invest £3000 for three years.
The Bank of Fixed Income Security offers the following accounts.

FLEXIBLE SHARE ACCOUNT	CASH INSTANT ISA ACCOUNT
3.5 % per annum	2.5 % per annum
simple interests	Compound interest

Work out which account offers Timothy the most income and by how much.
You must show your work.

(Total for question 4 is 4 marks)

9

(a) Expand and simplify $(2x - 1)^2(x + 4)$.

----

(2)

(b) Find the value of n

$$2 \times \sqrt{8} = 4^n$$

----

(3)

(Total for question 9 is 5 marks)

10

A bag contains red and blue balls only.
The probability of picking a red ball is 0.32.
Tina takes a ball at random from the bag and puts the ball back into the bag.
Tim then takes another ball at random from the bag.

(a) What is the probability that they take different coloured ball ?

----

(2)

(b) What assumption has been made to calculate the answer in part (a)?

----

(1)

(Total for question 10 is 3 marks)

11

Jason makes an 18*l* drink by mixing orange juice, pineapple juice and sparkling water in the ratio of 4 : 3 : 2.

Sparkling waters are sold in 750*ml* bottles, each costing £1.44.
Orange and pineapple juices are sold in a litre bottle, each costing £1.46 and £2.99 respectively.

Jason sells all the drink he makes in 300*ml* glasses.
He sells each glass of juice at £1.08

Work out Jason's profit from his sales.

£ --

(5)

(Total for question 11 is 5 marks)

12

There are 1000 students in a school.
200 students travel to school by car.
150 students who travel by car are male.
450 student walk to school.
There are total of 550 male students
150 female students travel by bus.

(a) Draw a two way table to show this information.

(3)

(b) One person is chosen at random.
 (i) What is the probability that the person is male and takes the bus?

----

(1)

 (ii) What is the probability that the person travels by car or walks to school?

----

(1)

(Total for question 12 is 5 marks)

13

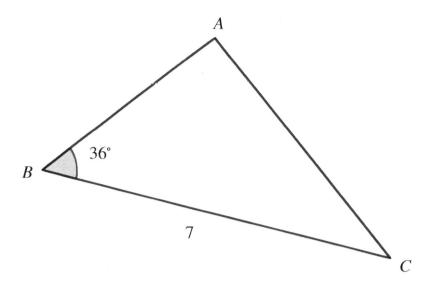

Triangle ABC has length $BC = 7$cm.

Size of the angle ABC : Size of the angle ACB

2 : 3

Angle $ABC = 36°$
Work out the area of the triangle.
Give your answer correct to one decimal place.

.... cm^2

(4)

(Total for question 13 is 4 marks)

14

Prove algebraically that the product of any two odd numbers is always an odd number.

(Total for question 14 is 3 marks)

15

Solve algebraically the simultaneous equations

$x^2 + 2y^2 = 14$
$y + 2x = 5$

Give your answer correct to three significant figures.

----

(5)

(Total for question 15 is 5 marks)

16

$$v^2 = u^2 + 2as$$

$a = 9.8$ correct to one decimal place
$s = 3.25$ correct to two decimal places
$v = -8.2$ correct to one decimal place

By considering bounds,
work out the upper and lower bound value of u correct to three significant figures.

Lower bound of u ....

Upper bound of u ....

(6)

(Total for question 16 is 6 marks)

17

Sketch the graphs of $y = \sin(x°)$, $\quad -180° \le x \le 180°$.

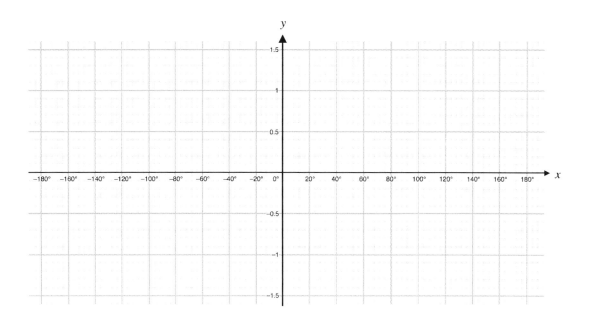

(Total for question 17 is 2 marks)

18

Fully simplify $\dfrac{1}{x-1} + \dfrac{2x^2+x}{x-1} \div \dfrac{4x^2+2x}{x^2-1}$

(Total for question 18 is 5 marks)

19

The graph has the equation of the form $y = ab^x$ and passes through the points $(0,2)$ and $(2,8)$.

Work out the value of the constants a and b where $a > 0, \; b > 0$.

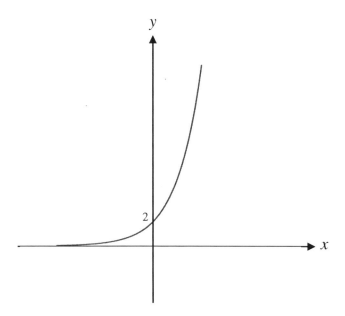

a --

b --

(3)

(Total for question 19 is 3 marks)

20

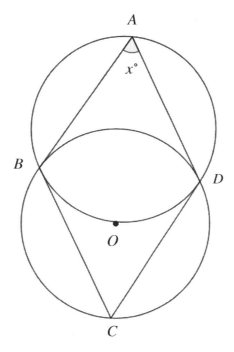

B, C, D are points on the circle centred at O. A, B, O and D are points on another circle.

Angle $B\hat{A}D = x°$

Show that $B\hat{C}D = 90 - \dfrac{1}{2}x$.

Give reasons for each stage of your answer.

(Total for question 20 is 4 marks)

End of the paper

Name _____

Surname_____

EDEXCEL GCSE Mathematics

Candidate Number

Centre Number

SET A Paper 3 (Calculator)

Higher Tier
Time allowed: 1 hour 30 minutes

Total marks: 80

Materials
You may use a calculator, ruler, eraser, compass, protractor, pen, pencil and tracing paper.

Instructions
- Answer all the questions.
- Answer each question on the space provided.
- Use of calculators is allowed.

Information
- The marks are shown for each question in the bracket.
- Method marks are given even if your answer is incorrect.
- Unless otherwise noted, diagrams are not drawn to scale.

Recommendations
- Read each question carefully.
- Check your answers thoroughly.

Answer ALL the questions.
Write your answers in the spaces provided.
Show all the steps of your calculation.

1   Sam truncated the length of his pencil l to 13.4cm, correct to one decimal place.
     Write down the error interval for his pencil l.

                                                      0.1
                                                      (2)

                                          (Total for question 1 is 2 marks)

2   Jacob buys 10kg tomatoes for £20.
     He makes tomato paste and puree in the ratio of 2 : 3.
     He sells them in 500g cans.

     He sells each can of paste at £1.50.
     He sells each can of puree at £2.
     Work out the percentage of profit he makes by selling all the paste and
     the puree.

                                                      %
                                                      (3)

                                          (Total for question 2 is 3 marks)

3   The table below shows the number of items that Jishan needs to send out to his customers.

	Up to 100g	Up to 250g	Up to 500g	Up to1kg	Up to 2kg
Small Letter	14	8			
Large Letter	5	9	3		
Small Parcel				7	4
Medium Parcel				9	3

The table below shows the prices charged by his delivery company.

Direct mail delivery charges

		1st Class Price	2nd Class Price
Small Letter	Up to 100g	£2.25	£2.06
	Up to 250g	£2.34	£2.17
Large Letter	Up to 100g	£2.69	£2.36
	Up to 250g	£3.23	£2.93
	Up to 500g	£3.79	£3.39
Small Parcel	Up to1kg	£4.85	£4.20
	Up to 2kg	£6.57	£4.20
Medium Parcel	Up to1kg	£7.00	£6.30
	Up to 2kg	£10.02	£6.30

He sends all the small letters using first-class stamps and large letters using second-class stamps.
(a) Work out the total cost of sending all of the letters.

----

(2)

He sends all his small and medium parcels under 1*kg* using the second-class stamps.
He sends the remaining parcels using first-class stamps.
(b) Work out the total cost of sending the parcels.

----

(2)

(c) How much money can he save if he sends all his letters and parcels by second-class stamp? Show your work.

----

(3)

(Total for question 3 is 7 marks)

4   Shape **A** is reflected on the line $x = 4$ to give shape **B**.
Shape **B** is reflected on the line $y = 2$ to give shape **C**.

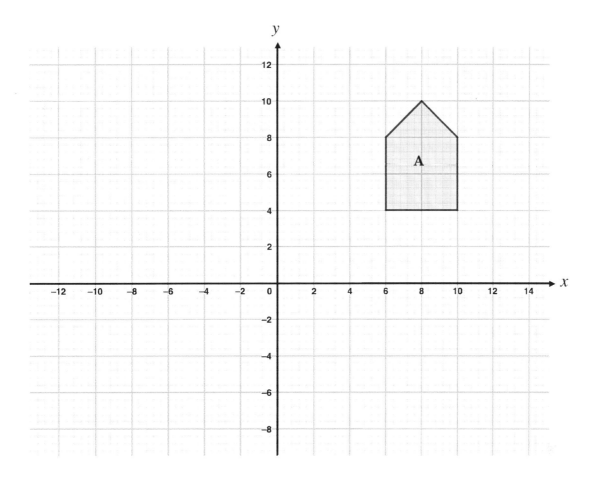

Describe the single transformation that maps shape **A** to Shape **C**.

....

....

(3)

(Total for question 4 is 3 marks)

5   In a company, the ratio between sales representatives and operation
     employees is 8 : 5.
     The ratio between operation employees and finance department
     employees is 10 : 7.

     There are 28 finance department employees in the company.
     How many sales representatives are there in the company?

     ----

                                                         (3)

                              (Total for question 5 is 3 marks)

6   Find the lowest common multiple of 6×10^{12} and 8×10^{22}.
Give your answer in standard form.

----

(3)

(Total for question 6 is 3 marks)

7   Ruby collected information about breaths and heartbeats per minute of her 10 friends after a quick running exercise.

She plotted that information on the scatter diagram below.

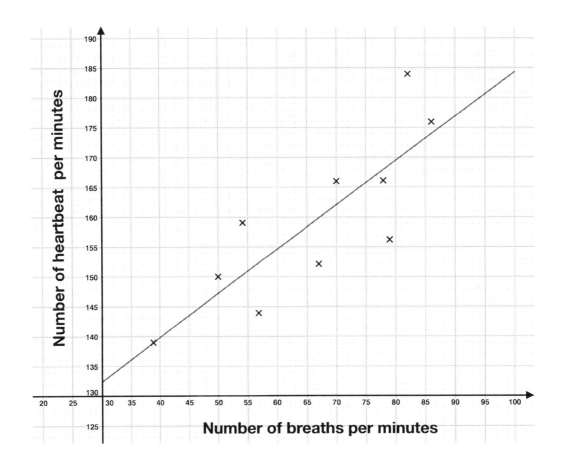

(a) Describe the type of correlation shown by the scatter diagram.

----

(1)

(b) Describe the relationship between breaths per minute and heart beats per minute after the exercise.

----

(1)

(c) Interpret the meaning of the gradient in the line of best fit.

----

(1)

(Total for question 7 is 3 marks)

8 An object has a mass of $5kg$ and a volume of $120cm^3$.
Mass is increased by 20%.
Volume is decreased by 50%.
Calculate the percentage change in density of the object.
Show all the steps of your calculation.

-- %

(3)

(Total for question 8 is 3 marks)

9 The nth term of sequence P_n is $2n^2 - 21n + 9$.
(a) Find the first three terms of this sequence.

----

(1)

The nth term of sequence Q_n is $6n - 4$.
(b) Work out the common terms of the sequence P_n and Q_n with the same term number.

----

(2)

(Total for question 9 is 3 marks)

10   The angles of a triangle are in the ratio $1 : 2 : 3$.
Its sides are in the ratio $1 : \sqrt{3} : 2$.
Its longest side is $25cm$.
Work out the exact area of the triangle.

cm^2
----

(3)

(Total for question 10 is 3 marks)

---

11   (a) Factorise $x^2 - 4x + 3$

(b) Simplify fully $(4\pi + 1)^2 - (4\pi - 1)^2$

(2)

----

(3)

(Total for question 11 is 5 marks)

12   The number of an ant population at the start of the year t is denoted p_t.
The ant population decreases by 12 % each year.

(a) Write down the expression of the ant population at the start of $t + 1$ year.

----

(2)

The initial ant population was 2000.

(b) Calculate the ant population at the end of the third year.
Give your answer to a suitable degree of accuracy.

----

(3)

(Total for question 12 is 5 marks)

13

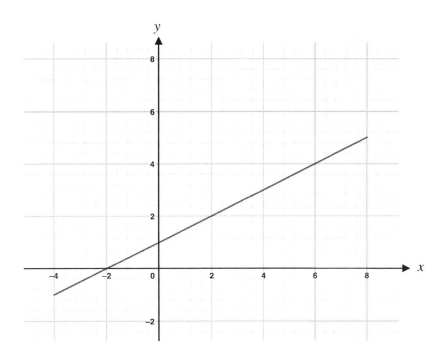

(a) Find the equation of the straight line l shown in the digram above.

----

(3)

(b) Find the equation of the line which is perpendicular to line l and passes through the point $(-2,6)$.

----

(3)

(Total for question 13 is 6 marks)

14 The cumulative frequency graph gives information about the GCSE maths tests.

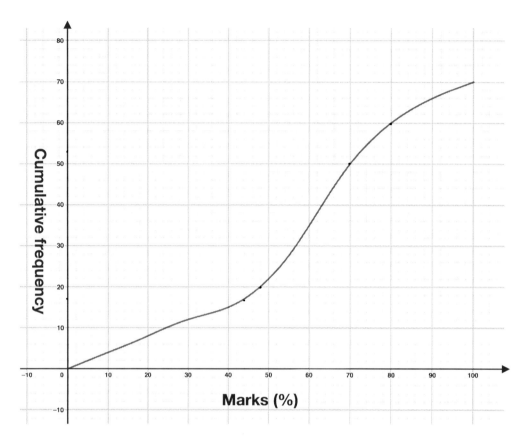

Use the cumulative frequency graph to estimate

(a) The median mark

_____ 60 _____ %

(1)

(b) The interquartile range

42   7

_____ 2 9 _____ %

(2)

The pass mark was 48%.

(c) Estimate how many students passed the test.

_____50_____

(1)

Given that the mark for getting level 7 was 70% to 80%:

(d) Estimate the percentage of students who achieved level 7.

_____10_____

(2)

(Total for question 14 is 6 marks)

15

Write $3x^2 - 12x + 13$ in the form $a(x-b)^2 + c$ where a, b and c are.

$$3(x-2) + 1$$

(3)

(Total for question 15 is 3 marks)

16 The diagram shows the equation of line $y = x - 1$ has been rotated 360 degrees between $x = 1$ and $x = 5$ to generate a solid cone. All measurements are in cm.

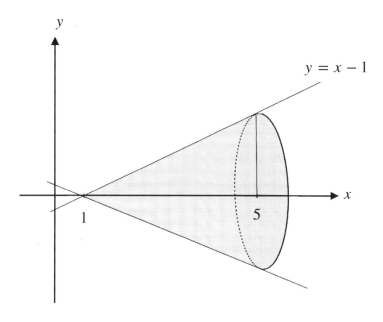

(a) Find the exact volume of the cone.

....

(2)

(b) Show that surface area of the cone is $16\pi\left(\sqrt{2}+1\right)$.

(4)

(Total for question 16 is 6 marks)

17

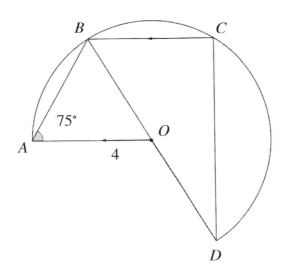

A, B, C, D are points on the circumference of the circle centred at O.
Lines OA and CB are parallel.
Line BD is a diameter of the circle and CD is a straight line.

Radius OA is $4cm$.
Angle $OAB = 75°$.

Show that the area of triangle BCD is $8\sqrt{3}$.

- -

(5)

(Total for question 17 is 5 marks)

18 The table shows information about the time, in minutes, that a group of people took to solve a sudoku problem.

Time in minutes	Frequency
$0 < t \leq 6$	3
$6 < t \leq 10$	8
$10 < t \leq 12$	5
$12 < t \leq 15$	12
$15 < t \leq 20$	3

(a) Use the information on the table to complete the histogram.

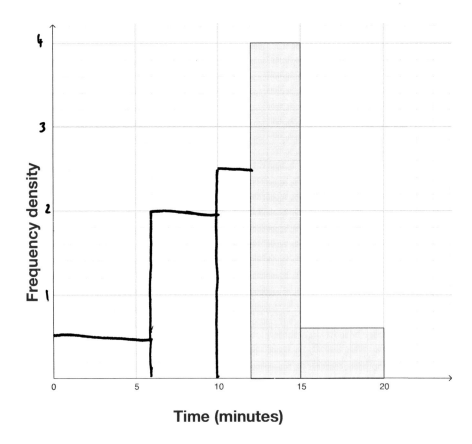

Time (minutes)

(2)

(b) Use the histogram to find the median time to solve the sudoku problem.

(2)

(c) Find the percentage of people who took between 11 and 13 minutes to solve the sudoku problem.

_____ %

(2)

(Total for question 18 is 6 marks)

19 Sophie invested £7,500 in the stock market.

The value of her investment increased by x % during the first year and by $\frac{1}{4}x$ % in the second year.

The value of her investment at the end of the second year was £8456.25.

Work out the value of x.

.... %

(5)

(Total for question 19 is 5 marks)

End of the paper

Name _____   Surname_____

EDEXCEL GCSE Mathematics

Candidate Number

Centre Number

SET B Paper 1 (Non-Calculator)

Higher Tier
Time allowed: 1 hour 30 minutes

Total marks: 80

Materials
You may use a ruler, eraser, compass, protractor, pen, pencil and tracing paper.

Instructions
- Answer all the questions.
- Answer each question on the space provided.
- Use of calculators is not allowed.

Information
- The marks are shown for each question in the bracket.
- Method marks are given even if your answer is incorrect.
- Unless otherwise noted, diagrams are not drawn to scale.

Advice
- Read each question carefully.
- Check your answers thoroughly.

Answer ALL the questions.
Write your answers in the spaces provided.
Show all the steps of your calculation.

1

(a) Rearrange the following fractions in ascending order.

$$\frac{1}{2}, \quad \frac{4}{5}, \quad \frac{2}{3}$$

$$\frac{1}{2}, \quad \frac{2}{3}, \quad \frac{4}{5}$$

(2)

(b) Find the value of $\dfrac{7^{10} \times 7^{-4}}{7^4}$.

$7^2 \quad 49$

(2)

(Total for question 1 is 4 marks)

©Inspire Studies   70   Not to be copied

2

John buys 12 T-shirts to sell. He pays a total of £108 for the T-shirts.
He gives two T-shirts to his friend as a gift.

He sells the remaining T-shirts and makes an overall 10 % profit on his
purchase price. Work out the selling price of a T-shirt.

£ ....

(2)

(Total for question 2 is 2 marks)

3

The ages of two girls are in the ratio of 7 : 4.
Two years later, the ratio of their ages will be 8 : 5.
Find their present ages.

$$7 + 4 = 11 \Big) = 2$$
$$8 + 5 = 13$$

$$14 : 8$$
$$16 : 10$$

16   10

(3)

(Total for question 3 is 3 marks)

4

It takes six days for 20 people to finish a project.

(a) How many people are needed to complete the project in 2 days?

$$\underline{60}$$

(2)

(b) If 15 people worked on the project, how many days does it take to finish?

$$\frac{20}{6} = \frac{10}{3} \qquad \frac{10}{6.5}$$

$$\underline{4 \cdot 5}$$

(2)

(c) Write down one assumption you have made in part (b).

The people all work at the same speed

(1)

(Total for question 4 is 5 marks)

5

(a) Complete this table for $y = x^2 - 2x - 4$.

x	−2	−1	0	1	2	3	4
y	4	−1	−4	−5	−4	−1	4

1 + 2 -4

4 + 4 -4

(2)

(b) On the grid, draw the graph of $y = x^2 - 2x - 4$ for values of x from -2 to 4.

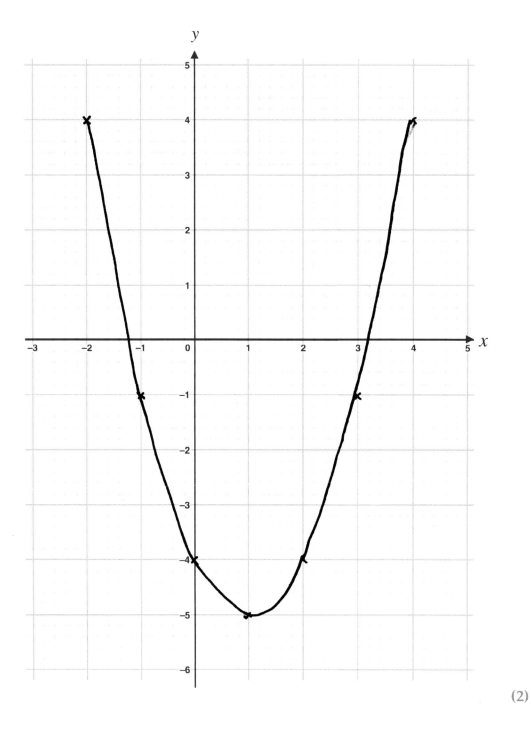

(2)

(c) Using the graph, estimate the solutions to $x^2 - 2x - 4 = 0$.

-1   1·2

16 +8

$x = -1.2$ $x = 3.2$

(1)

(Total for question 5 is 5 marks)

6

The cost of 3kg chicken, C, and 1kg mutton, M, is £11.
If 2kg chicken and 3kg mutton cost £19,

(a) Write the above information as a pair of linear equations.

$3C + M = 11$

$2C + 3M = 19$

(2)

(b) Find the cost of a kilogram of chicken and a kilogram of mutton.

Chicken £ ....

Mutton £ ....

(3)

(Total for question 6 is 5 marks)

7

The triangle ABC is reflected in the line $x = -1$ to give the shape $A'B'C'$.
The triangle $A'B'C'$ is reflected in the line $y = 2$ to give the shape $A''B''C''$.

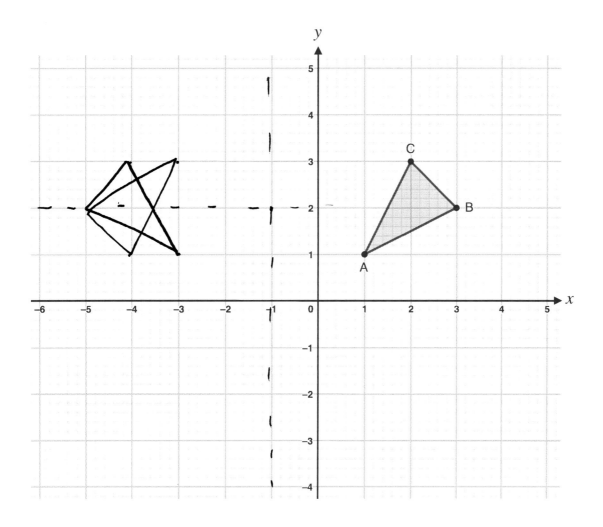

Describe fully the single transformation that will map the triangle ABC to the triangle $A''B''C''$.

Rotated 180° around (-1,2)

(4)

(Total for question 7 is 4 marks)

8

Thomas sells a bakery item.

The production cost of the item increased by 20%.

He keeps the item's selling price the same but reduces the weight to keep his production cost per item the same.

Work out the percentage decrease in the weight of the item.

Show all your work.

.... %

(3)

(Total for question 8 is 3 marks)

9

The table gives information about the ages of children in the playground.

Age in years	2	3	5	6	9	12
Frequency	3	5	2	4	2	3

(a) What is the modal age of the children in the playground ?

.... years

(1)

(b) Find the median age of the children in the playground.

.... years

(2)

(Total for question 9 is 3 marks)

10

A bag contains black and white identical marbles. Sina takes a marble at random from the bag.

The probability that the marble is white is 0.4.

Sina puts the marble back into the bag.

Albert takes a marble at random from the bag.

(a) Find the probability that Sina and Albert take marbles of the same colour.

----

(3)

(b) If the total number of marbles in the bag was 40, how many black marbles were there in the bag?

----

(1)

(Total for question 10 is 4 marks)

11

If $\mathbf{a} = \begin{pmatrix} 3 \\ 2 \end{pmatrix}$ and $\mathbf{b} = \begin{pmatrix} 9 \\ 6 \end{pmatrix}$ then,

(a) Show that $\mathbf{a}$ and $\mathbf{b}$ are parallel to each other.

(1)

(b) Find the exact magnitude of $\mathbf{a} + \mathbf{b}$.

Give your answer in its simplest form.

(3)

(Total for question 11 is 4 marks)

12

(a) Simplify fully $\dfrac{1}{a+b} + \dfrac{b}{a^2-b^2}$

----

(2)

(b) Factorise fully $45 - 5p^4$

----

(2)

(Total for question 12 is 4 marks)

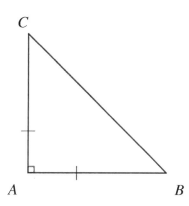

(a) The area of the right-angled isosceles triangle ABC is 18 cm².
   Find its exact perimeter.

_____ cm

(4)

(b) Write down the value of $\cos(60°)$.

_____

(1)

(Total for question 13 is 5 marks)

14

Prove that the square of every even number is divisible by 4.

- -

(3)

(Total for question 14 is 3 marks)

15

If $\sqrt{3}\left(\sqrt{18} + \sqrt{50}\right) = m\sqrt{6}$ where m is an integer, find the value of m.

$$m = \underline{\hspace{5cm}}$$

(3)

(Total for question 15 is 3 marks)

16

Given that $a = b^x, b = c^y, c = a^z,$

Show that $xyz = 1$.

$$\underline{\hspace{5cm}}$$

(3)

(Total for question 16 is 3 marks)

17

Find the integer values of n that satisfy the inequalities

$$-4 \geq \frac{10 - 2n}{5} \geq -6 \text{ and } \frac{n}{3} + 2 > 8$$

(5)

(Total for question 17 is 5 marks)

18

(a) Change $2.\dot{5}7\dot{6}$ into a fraction in its simplest form.

----

(3)

(b) Solve the quadratic equation below by completing the square.

$$4x^2 - 7x + 3 = 0$$

----

(3)

(Total for question 18 is 6 marks)

19

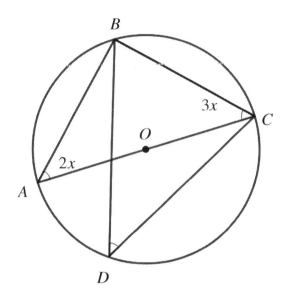

In the figure, O is the centre of the circle.
$C\hat{A}B = 2x°$ and $B\hat{C}A = 3x°$.
Find the value of the angle CDB.
Give reasons for each stage of your answer.

$C\hat{D}B = $ --

(4)

(Total for question 19 is 4 marks)

20

The table below shows information about the height in centimetre of plants at Richmond Nursery.

	Height (cm)
Median	9
Lower Quartile	8.5
Maximum Height	18
Interquartile Range	5.5
Range	11

(a) Draw a box plot for this information.

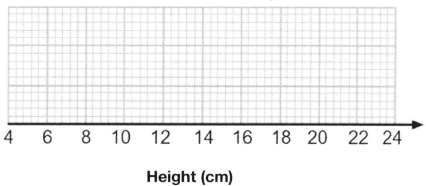

Richmond Nursery

Height (cm)

(3)

The box plot below shows information about the height in inches of plants at Petunia Nursery.

Petunia Nursery

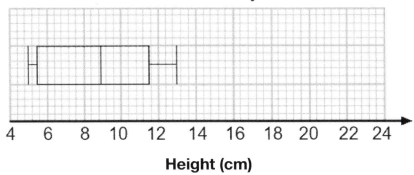

Height (cm)

(b) Compare the distribution of plant heights between the two nurseries.

----

(2)

(Total for question 20 is 5 marks)

End of the paper

General Certificate of Secondary Education

Name _____

Surname_____

EDEXCEL GCSE Mathematics

Candidate Number

Centre Number

SET B Paper 2 (Calculator)

Higher Tier
Time allowed: 1 hour 30 minutes

Total marks: 80

Materials
You may use a ruler, eraser, compass, protractor, pen, pencil and tracing paper.

Instructions
- Answer all the questions.
- Answer each question on the space provided.
- Use of calculators is allowed.

Information
- The marks are shown for each question in the bracket.
- Method marks are given even if your answer is incorrect.
- Unless otherwise noted, diagrams are not drawn to scale.

- Read each question carefully.
- Check your answers thoroughly.

Answer ALL the questions.
Write your answers in the spaces provided.
Show all the steps of your calculation.

1

Use your calculator to work out $\sqrt{\dfrac{\sin 50° - \sin 20°}{\sin 20° + \sin 50°}}$.

Give your answer to 3 decimal places.

----

(2)

(Total for question 1 is 2 marks)

2

(a) Solve $6x - 4 = 2(2x - 4)$

----

(2)

(b) Expand and fully simplify $3x - (x - 3)^2$

----

(2)

(Total for question 2 is 4 marks)

3

Ronald had £160. He distributed 75% of that amount to his son and daughter in the ratio 2 : 3.

Find the amount of money his son received.
Show each stage of your work.

£ _____

(2)

(Total for question 3 is 2 marks)

4

Sima asked her sister Dina to write a 3-digit number such that the sum of the first two digits is 14 and the third digit is positive multiple of 2.

Dina said,
"I can write 20 different such numbers." Is Dina correct?
Justify your answer.

(Total for question 4 is 2 marks)

5

A department store provides two offers:

Offer 1: "Take a 20% discount on total purchase and pay 15% tax."
Offer 2: "First pay 10% tax and take 15% discount on the total purchase."

Adam wants to purchase goods worth £420.
Which option offers him the best value for money?
Justify your answer.

(Total for question 5 is 4 marks)

6 James has 42 pens and 18 pencils.
He wants to distribute these pens and pencils to his students such that each student gets the same number of pens and the same number of pencils.

(a) What is the greatest number of student James can distribute pen and pencil? Show each stage of your answer.

students

....

(2)

Pens are sold in packs of 42.
Pencils are sold in packs of 18.
David wants to buy an equal number of pens and pencils.
(b) Work out the smallest number of packs of pens and pencils he needs to buy. Show how you get your answer.

Packs of pencils   ....

Packs of pens   ....

(2)

(Total for question 6 is 4 marks)

7

Albert has 16 rare stamps.
He decided to start a stamp collection the following month. He added five new stamps to his collection each month.

(a) At the end of how many months, Albert had 166 stamps?
Show how you get your answer.

.... months

(2)

(b) Is it possible for him to collect 297 stamps?
Give a reason for your answer.

----

(1)

(Total for question 7 is 3 marks)

8

The diameter of Joseph's bicycle tyre is 70 cm.

(a) Find the exact circumference of the tyre.

----------------------------------- cm

(1)

Joseph travelled 11 km with that bicycle.
(b) Find the total number of revolutions of the tyre.

----

(2)

(Total for question 8 is 3 marks)

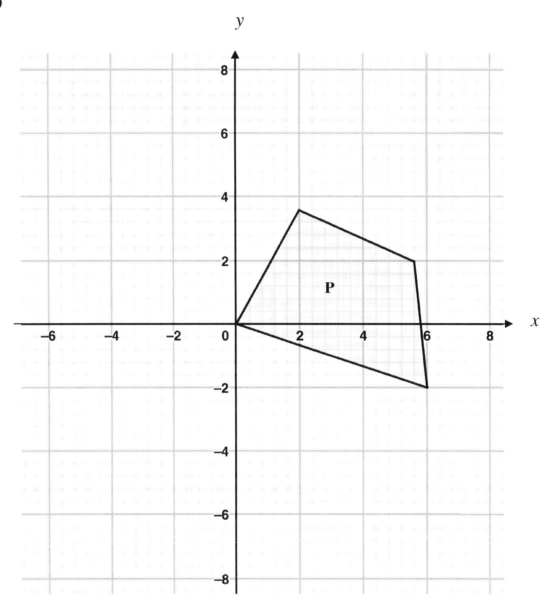

(a) Rotate quadrilateral **P** about the origin by 90° anticlockwise and label the new shape **P₁**.

(2)

(b) Reflect $\mathbf{P_1}$ on $y = 0$ and label new shape $\mathbf{P_2}$.

(2)

(c) Describe the single transformation that will map shape $\mathbf{P}$ to shape $\mathbf{P_2}$.

----

(2)

(d) Write down the coordinate of the invariant point.

----

(1)

(Total for question 9 is 7 marks)

10

In a school, the ratio of teachers to the student is 1: 25.
The ratio of boys to girls is 4: 5.
There are 250 girls in the school.

(a) Find the number of students

----

(2)

(b) Find the total number of teachers.

----

(1)

The mean weight of a group of boys is $(19 + 2m)$, and the sum of their weight is $(1330 + 140m)$.
(c) Find the total number of boys.

----

(2)

(Total for question 10 is 5 marks)

11

A bag contains 21 red marbles and 15 white marbles.
Jofra draws a marble at random, records its colour, returns to the bag, and draws a marble again.

(a) Draw a complete tree diagram to show all the probabilities for these two marbles.

(3)

(b) Find the probability that both marbles are of the same colour.

(1)

(Total for question 11 is 4 marks)

12

C is the point with coordinates $(4, m + 1)$.
D is the point with coordinate $(2m + 3, 3)$.
The gradient of line CD is 1.

(a) Work out the value of m.

$m =$ ------------------------------------

(2)

(b) Find the equation of the line CD.

----

(2)

(Total for question 12 is 4 marks)

13

Anthony wants to find two positive consecutive multiples of 5 such that their product is 300.

Anthony supposes the first number is $(x - 5)$.
(a) Write down another number as an expression of x?

----

(1)

(b) Find the value of the two numbers.

----

(3)

(Total for question 13 is 4 marks)

14

Forty thousand students are registered in a university.
The number of students increases by 5% every year.

(a) Find the time in years when the total number of students is 46305.

.... years

(2)

Jim says,
    "Total percentage increase in student numbers over three years is 15%,
    Since the student number increases by 5% each year."

(b) Is he correct? Give your reason.

----

(1)

(Total for question 14 is 3 marks)

15

The following table shows the percentage of marks obtained by 200 students in an examination.

Marks (%)	Number of students
$10 < m \leq 20$	45
$20 < m \leq 30$	25
$30 < m \leq 40$	56
$40 < m \leq 50$	44
$50 < m \leq 60$	p

(a) Find the value of p

$p =$ ------------------------------------

(1)

(b) Draw a cumulative frequency graph to show this result on the grid below.

(2)

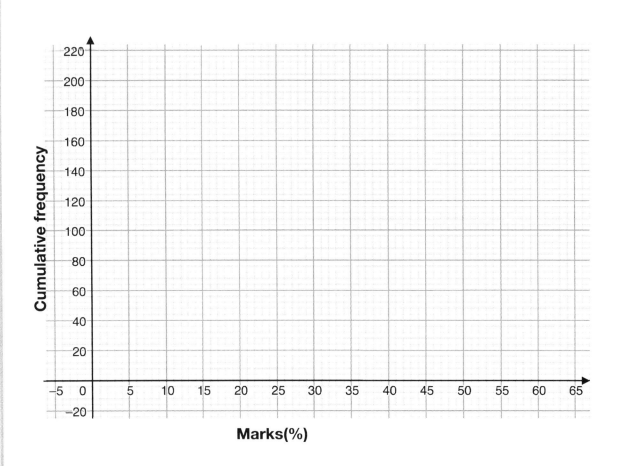

50% of students passed the exam.

(c) Use your graph to estimate the pass mark.

_____ %

(1)

(Total for question 15 is 4 marks)

16

    Some students planned a weekend ski trip with a total budget of £4200.
    Five students cannot go on the trip. The cost of the trip is increased by
    £70 for each student.

(a) Taking the number of total students as x, and the cost for each student
     as y, write the pair of equations representing this problem.

----

(2)

(b) Find how many students went on the ski trip. Show all your work.

-------------------------------- students

(4)

(Total for question 16 is 6 marks)

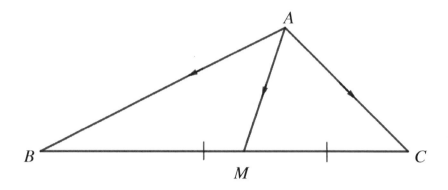

In the given figure, AM is the median of triangle ABC.

(a) Write equal but opposite vector to $\overrightarrow{BM}$.

----

(1)

(b) Prove that $\overrightarrow{AM} = \dfrac{1}{2}\left(\overrightarrow{AB} + \overrightarrow{AC}\right)$

----

(3)

(Total for question 17 is 4 marks)

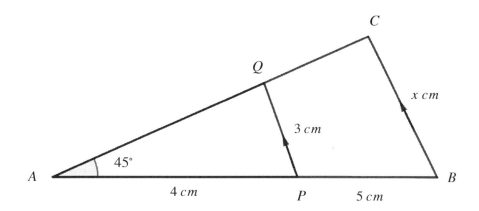

In the figure PQ is parallel to BC
$AP = 4\,cm, PB = 5\,cm$
$PQ = 3\,cm, BC = x\,cm$
$Q\hat{A}P = 45°$

(a) Find the value of x

cm

----

(2)

(b) Find the area of the triangle AQP. Give your answer correct
to two decimal place

cm^2

----

(3)

(Total for question 18 is 5 marks)

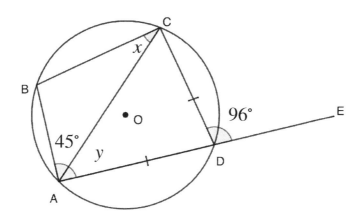

19

In the following figure
$AD = CD$
$B\hat{A}C = 45°$
$C\hat{D}E = 96°$

(a) Find the value of x and y.
  Give a reason for each stage of your answer.

$x =$ .... $y =$ ....

(4)

(b) What is the relationship between angles ABC and ADC ?

----

(1)

(Total for question 19 is 5 marks)

20    $f(x) = 3x + 6$ and $g(x) = x^2 - 2$

(a) Find the value of $fg(4)$

$fg(4) =$ _____

(2)

Given that $f(a) = 2b$ and $g(a) = b$

(b) Find the value of a and b. Give your answer to
one decimal place.

$a =$ .... $b =$ ....

(3)

(Total for question 20 is 5 marks)

End of the paper

Name _____   Surname_____

EDEXCEL GCSE Mathematics

Candidate Number

Centre Number

SET B Paper 3 (Calculator)

Higher Tier
Time allowed: 1 hour 30 minutes

Total marks: 80

Materials

You may use a ruler, eraser, compass, protractor, pen, pencil and tracing paper.

Instructions
- Answer all the questions.
- Answer the question on the spaces provided.
- Use of calculators is allowed.

Information
- The marks are shown for each question in the bracket.
- Method marks are given even if your answer is incorrect.
- Unless otherwise noted, diagrams are not drawn to scale.

Advice
- Read each question carefully.
- Check your answers thoroughly.

Answer ALL questions.
Write your answers in the spaces provided.
Show all the steps of your calculation.

1

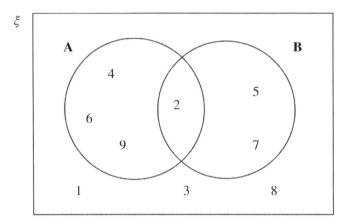

Simon asked Lily to choose a number from the universal set ξ at random.

(a) Calculate the probability that Lily chooses a number that is not an element of B.

----

(1)

(b) Tom calculates the probability of $A \cup B$ as $P(A \cup B) = \dfrac{4}{9} + \dfrac{3}{9} = \dfrac{7}{9}$

Is he correct? Justify your answer.

----

(1)

(Total for question 1 is 2 marks)

2

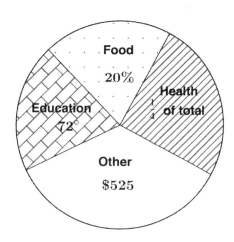

The following pie chart shows one months' expense of Justin's family.

(a) Find the percentage of total expense in Health and Education.

....

(2)

(b) Find the total expense for the month.

$ ....

(2)

(Total for question 2 is 4 marks)

3

Harry wants to buy honey. The price list for different amount is given in the table.

100 grams	200 grams	450 grams
£1.5	£2.5	£5

(a) Which option is the best value for money? Show your work.

----

(3)

Honey is sold only as a whole jar. Harry wants to buy 1.5 kg honey.
(b) Show how he could buy it at the lowest cost.
    You must justify your answer.

(3)

(Total for question 3 is 6 marks)

4

Three students ,X Y, Z, share some money.
The ratio of money X gets to the money Y get is 3: 4.
The ratio of the money Y gets to the money Z get is 2 : 3.
Given that Z gets £12 more than X.

(a) Work out the total amount of money.

£ --

(2)

(b) Find how much money each of the students gets.

Z --

Y --

X --

(2)

(Total for question 4 is 4 marks)

5

Hasim tosses a fair coin and then rolls a fair six-sided dice,

(a) Draw a sample space diagram showing all the possible combinations of outcomes.

(2)

(b) Use your sample space diagram to find the probability of getting an even number on the dice and head on a coin.

----

(1)

(Total for question 5 is 3 marks)

6

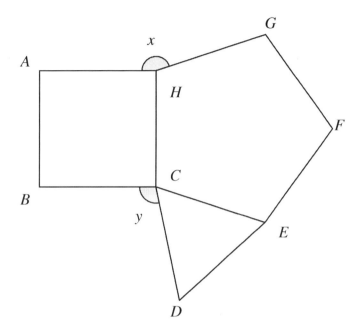

The diagram shows an equilateral triangle, a square and a regular pentagon.
Calculate the size of the angle x and angle y.
You must show all your work.

$x =$ ------------------------------------

$y =$ ------------------------------------

(3)

(Total for question 6 is 3 marks)

7

The initial number of bacteria in a petri dish is 2.3×10^8

The number of bacteria decreases by 10% each day.

(a) Find the number of bacteria after three days.

Give your answer in standard form correct to 3 significant figures.

----

(3)

Nasim says,

"With a 10% decrease, the number of bacteria in the petri dish is never zero."

(b) Is this statement correct? Explain your answer.

----

(1)

(Total for question 7 is 4 marks)

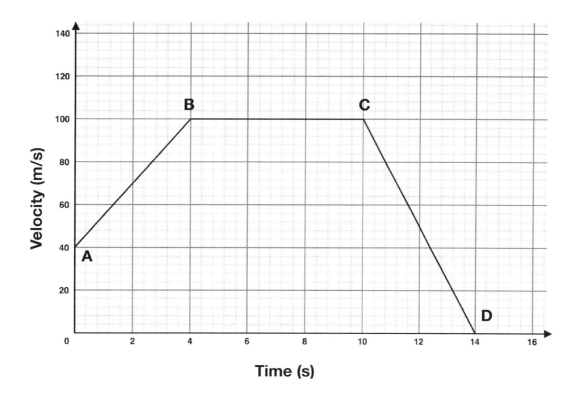

8

The velocity-time graph of a train is given in the graph.
(a) Find the acceleration of the train from A to B.

_____ m/s^2

(2)

Rekha said,

" Since the velocity from A to B is constant, acceleration is also constant."

(b) Is she correct? Explain your answer.

----

(1)

(c) Find the total distance traveled by the train from point A to D.

-------------------------------- Meters

(3)

(Total for question 8 is 6 marks)

9

Tonish is trying to find the value of π using the identity

$$\pi = \frac{A}{r^2}$$

Given that,
$A = 616\,cm^2$ correct nearest centimetre.
$r = 14\,cm$ to the nearest centimetre.

Work out the upper bound and lower bound value of π.
Give your answer correct to 3 significant figures.

Lower bound of π

Upper bound of π

----

(4)

(Total for question 9 is 4 marks)

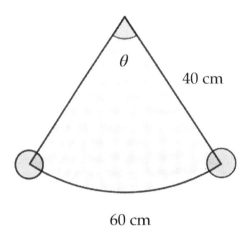

10

Sonia is conducting a physics experiment on pendulum motion.
Her 40 cm pendulum traverses an arc of 60 cm, as shown in the diagram.
(a) Find the angle of rotation, θ of the pendulum.
    Give your answer in terms of π

$\theta =$

----

(2)

(b) Work out the exact total area covered by the pendulum.

cm^2

----

(2)

(Total for question 10 is 4 marks)

11

Buildings A and B are 35 meters apart across the street from each other on the same horizontal ground.

The angle of elevation from the point on top of building A to the top of building B is 24°.
The angle of depression to the base of building B is 34°.

Work out the height of each building.
Show your work and give your answer correct to one decimal place.

meters

----

(4)

(Total for question 11 is 4 marks)

12

See the following quadratic sequence

3, 10, 19, 30, 43

(a) Write the following two numbers in that sequence.

----------------------------------   ----------------------------

(1)

(b) Find the nth term of this sequence.

----

(3)

(c) Using the answer to part (b), find the 10th term of the sequence.

----

(1)

(Total for question 12 is 5 marks)

13

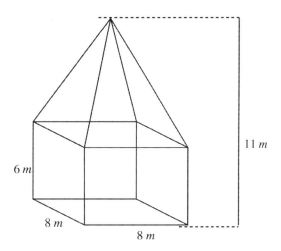

11 m

6 m

8 m

8 m

Tony builds a shed that is in the shape of a cuboid surmounted by a square-based pyramid.
He wants to paint the outer surface of the shed.
The cost of painting is £2.15 per square meter.
Work out the total cost of painting the shed? Show all your work.

£

....

(4)

(Total for question 13 is 4 marks)

14

Make x the subject of $y - 2 = \sqrt{\dfrac{x + 4}{x - m}}$

(3)

(Total for question 14 is 3 marks)

15

(a) Solve the inequality $x^2 - x - 20 \leq 0$.

----

(2)

(b) Show your answer to part (a) on the number line below.

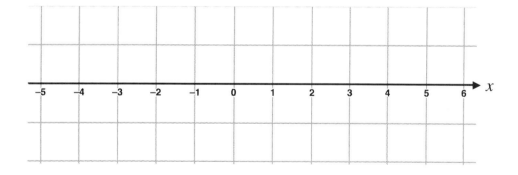

(1)

(Total for question 15 is 3 marks)

16

The sum of Naved's age and his younger brother's age is 17 years.
The sum of squares of their ages is 149 years.
Work out the ages of Naved and his brother.
Show all your work

Naved's age   Years

His brother's age   Years
----

(4)

(Total for question 16 is 4 marks)

17

(a) Show that the equation $x^3 - 5x - 4 = 0$ has a solution between 0 and 3.

(1)

(b) Show that the equation $x^3 - 5x - 4 = 0$ can be rearranged as

$$x = \sqrt{5 + \frac{4}{x}}$$

(2)

(c) Starting with $x_0 = 1$, use the iteration formula,

$$x_{n+1} = \sqrt{5 + \frac{4}{x_n}}$$

to find the solution of $x^3 - 5x - 4 = 0$ correct to 2 decimal place.
Show all your work

$x =$

----

(3)

(Total for question 17 is 6 marks)

18

The following figure is the sketch of the curve $y = f(x)$

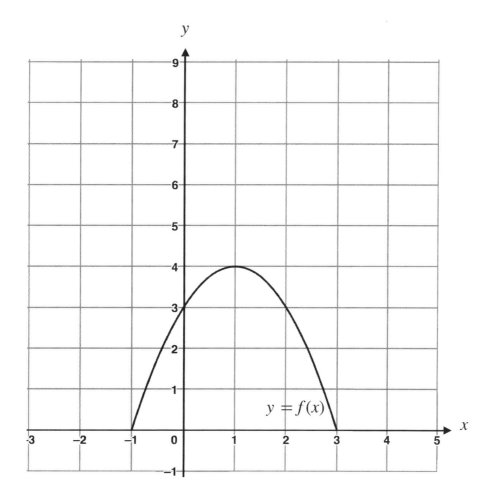

(a) Sketch the curve $y = 2f(x)$ on the same axes.

(3)

(b) State the equation of the line of symmetry of $y = -f(x)$

----

(1)

(Total for question 18 is 4 marks)

19

The histogram shows information about the year 11 maths test score.

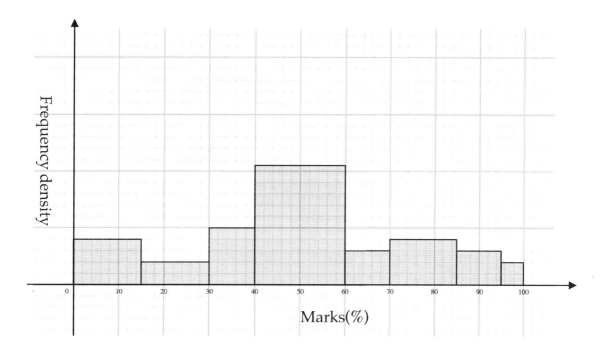

Marks(%)

Three students scored between 60% to 70%

(a) Complete the frequency table using the histogram

Marks (%)	Frequency
$0 < n \leq 15$	
$15 < n \leq 30$	
$30 < n \leq 40$	
$40 < n \leq 60$	
$60 < n \leq 70$	3
$70 < n \leq 85$	
$85 < n \leq 95$	
$95 < n \leq 100$	

(3)

(b) Use the histogram to estimate the median mark.

%

- -

(2)

The pass mark for the test was 34%.

(c) Using the histogram, estimate how many people passed the test

----

(2)

(Total for question 19 is 7 marks)

End of the paper

SET A-Paper 1 Solutions

1. $\dfrac{2^4 \times 2}{2^8 \times 2^0} = \dfrac{2^5}{2^8} = \dfrac{1}{2^3} = \dfrac{1}{8}$ **(1 mark)**

2. (a) $mx = y - c,\quad x = \dfrac{y-c}{m}$ **(1 mark)**

    (b) $x = \dfrac{10 - (-4)}{-2} = \dfrac{14}{-2} = -7$ **(1 mark)**

3. $180°$ rotation about the point $(1,1)$ **(2 marks)**
Or
Enlargement by scale factor -1 about the point $(1,1)$.

4. (a) $J:M = 4:3 \quad M:A = 5:8,$
      $J:M = 20:15 \quad M:A = 15:24$ **(1 mark)**
      Therefore $J:M:A = 20:15:24,$
      $J:A = 5:6$ **(1 mark)**

    (b) $2000 \div 20 = 100,$
      Mark
      $15 \times 100 = 1500$
      Annie
      $24 \times 100 = 2400$
      Annie has the highest monthly salary.

                                 (2 marks)

5. $8 \times 4 = 32,\ \dfrac{4 \times 4}{2} = 8,\quad \dfrac{1}{4} \times \pi \times 4^2 = 4\pi$ **(2 marks)**

    $32 - 8 - 4\pi = 24 - 4\pi$ **(2 marks)**

    $\dfrac{24 - 4\pi}{4\pi} = \dfrac{\cancel{4}(6 - \pi)}{\cancel{4}\pi} = \dfrac{6 - \pi}{\pi}$ **(1 mark)**

6. (a) $\dfrac{\sqrt{3}}{2}$ **(1 mark)**

    (b) $\sin(30°) = \dfrac{x}{50},$
      $x = \sin(30°) \times 50 = \dfrac{1}{2} \times 50 = 25$ **(2 marks)**

7. (a) $\dfrac{\cancel{(x+1)}(x+2)}{2(x+1)\cancel{^2}} = \dfrac{x+2}{2(x+1)}$ **(1 mark)**

    (b) $162 - 2k^2$
      $= 2\left(81 - k^2\right)$
      $= 2\left(9^2 - k^2\right)$
      $= 2(9 - k)(9 + k)$ **(2 marks)**

8. (a)

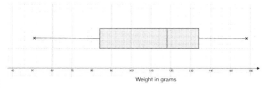

Weight in grams

      Upper quartile = lower quartile + interquartile range
      $84 + 50 = 134$ **(3 marks)**

    (b) Median tomatoes this year were higher than last year.

The interquartile ranger for both distribution were about the same.
Any two valid comparison of measure of spreads, averages and quartiles.   **(2 marks)**

9. (a)

Number of taps	Number of tanks	Time in hours
3	5	4
1	5	$4 \times 3 = 12$
1	5	$\dfrac{4 \times 3}{2} = 6$

      $6 \times 60 = 360$ minutes   **(2 marks)**

    (b) All tap fills the tank at the same rate.
Or
All tanks have the same volume.

                                    (1 mark)

(c)

Number of tanks	Time in hours	Number of taps
5	4	3
1	4	$\dfrac{3}{5}$
8	4	$\dfrac{3}{5} \times 8$
8	$\dfrac{4}{4} = 1$	$\dfrac{3 \times 8}{5} \times 4 = \dfrac{96}{5}$
8	$1 \times 6 = 6$	$\dfrac{3 \times 8}{5 \times 6} \times 4 = 3\tfrac{1}{5} \approx 4$

                                    (3 marks)

10. $1.\dot{4} = 1 + 0.444\ldots$
    Let $x = 0.44444\ldots$
    $10x = 4.444\ldots$
    $x = 0.4444\ldots$ **(1 mark)**

    $- - - - - - - - - - - - - - - - - - - -$

    $9x = 4$ (Subtract x from $10x$ and $0.444\ldots$ from $4.444\ldots$)
    $x = \dfrac{4}{9}$ **(1 mark)**
    Hence
    $1.\dot{4} = 1 + \dfrac{4}{9} = 1\tfrac{4}{9} = \dfrac{13}{9}$ **(1 mark)**

11. (a) $\left(\dfrac{64}{343}\right)^{\frac{2}{3}} = \dfrac{(\sqrt[3]{64})^2}{(\sqrt[3]{343})^2} = \dfrac{4^2}{7^2} = \dfrac{16}{49}$

                                    (2 marks)

(b) $7^1 \times 7^{\frac{1}{2}} = 7^{\frac{3}{2}} = 7^x$, $\quad x = \dfrac{3}{2}$,

$\dfrac{1}{7\sqrt{7}} = 7^{-\frac{3}{2}} = 7^{y-2}$,

$y - 2 = -\dfrac{3}{2}$ $\quad y = \dfrac{1}{2}$ **(2 marks)**

$\dfrac{\frac{3}{2} \times \frac{1}{2}}{3} = \dfrac{1}{4}$ **(1 mark)**

12. $\dfrac{(\sqrt{4} \times \sqrt{3} - \sqrt{3})^2}{\sqrt{3}+1} = \dfrac{(\sqrt{3})^2}{\sqrt{3}+1} = \dfrac{3}{\sqrt{3}+1}$

(1 mark)

$\dfrac{3}{\sqrt{3}+1} \times \dfrac{\sqrt{3}-1}{\sqrt{3}-1} = \dfrac{3\sqrt{3}-3}{2} = -\dfrac{3}{2} + \dfrac{3}{2}\sqrt{3}$ **(1 mark)**

$a = -\dfrac{3}{2}$, $\quad b = \dfrac{3}{2}$ **(1 mark)**

13. $A : B$
$16\pi : 36\pi$
$16 : 36$
$4 : 9$ (Area scale factors)
$\sqrt{4} : \sqrt{9}$
$2 : 3$ (Radius/length scale factors) **(1 mark)**
$A : B : C$
$2 : 3 : 4$ (Radius scale factors) **(1 mark)**
$A : C$
$2 : 4$
$1 : 2$ (Radius scale factor between A and C)
$1^3 : 2^3$
$1 : 8$ (Volume scale factor between A and C)

(1 mark)

14. (a) $fg(x) = (2(x-1) - 1)^2$ (Substitute $g(x)$ into $f(x)$)
$= (2x-3)^2$ **(1 mark)**
$= (2x-3)(2x-3)$
$= 4x^2 - 12x + 9$ **(1 mark)**
$a = 4, b = -12, c = 9$ **(1 mark)**

(b) $fg(x) = 9$
$4x^2 - 12x + 9 = 9$
$4x^2 - 12x = 0$ **(1 mark)**
$4x(x - 3) = 0$
$4x = 0$ or $x - 3 = 0$
$x = 0$ or $x = 3$ **(1 mark)**

15. $c = -1$ **(1 mark)**
(graphs crosses the y axis at -1)
$a(-2)^2 + b(-2) - 1 = 0$
(Graph crosses the x axis at ($-2,0$))
$4a - 2b - 1 = 0$
$4a - 2b = 1$ (equation 1)

$a(6)^2 + 6b - 1 = 0$ (Graph crosses the x axis at $(6, 0)$)
$36a + 6b = 1$ (equation 2)
$12a - 6b = 3$ **(1 mark)**
(multiply equation 1 by 3 and add to equation 2)

$48a = 4, a = \dfrac{4}{48} = \dfrac{1}{12}$ **(1 mark)**

$4\left(\dfrac{1}{12}\right) - 2b = 1$ Substitute value of a into equation 1.

$\dfrac{1}{3} - 2b = 1, 2b = -\dfrac{2}{3}, b = -\dfrac{1}{3}$ **(1 mark)**

Alternative method:
x intercept of the graphs is at -2 and 6.
Therefore $y = a(x + 2)(x - 6)$ for some constant a.
y intercept is at -1 so,
$a \times (2) \times (-6) = -1$ and $a = \frac{1}{12}$ **(1mark)**
$y = \frac{1}{12}(x + 2)(x - 6)$
$= \frac{1}{12}(x^2 - 4x - 12)$
$= \frac{1}{12}x^2 - \frac{4}{12}x - \frac{12}{12}$
$= \frac{1}{12}x^2 - \frac{1}{3}x - 1$ **(1 mark)**
Hence,
$a = \frac{1}{12}, b = -\frac{1}{3}, c = -1$ **(1 mark)**

16. $A\hat{O}C = 2 \times A\hat{B}C = 2 \times 70 = 140$ **(1 mark)**
(Angles on centre is twice the angle on circumference)

$O\hat{A}F = O\hat{C}F = 90°$ **(1 mark)**
(Radius meets the angle at 90°)

$x = 360° - 90° - 90° - 140° = 40°$ **(2 marks)**
(Angles on the quadrilateral $AOCF$ add up to 360°)

17. (a)

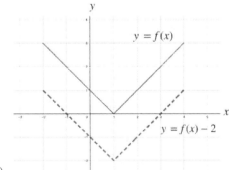

(2 marks)

(b) $h(x - 2)$ **(1 mark)**

18. $x^2 < 16$
$x^2 - 16 < 0$
$(x - 4)(x + 4) < 0$
$-4 < x < 4)$ **(2 marks)**

$$\frac{8-x}{2} < x+1$$
$$8-x < 2x+2$$
$$6 < 3x$$
$$x > 2 \qquad \textbf{(2 marks)}$$

$$x = 3 \qquad \textbf{(1 mark)}$$

19. $y = ku$ for some constant value k
$8 = 4k, k = 2$ so $y = 2u$ **(1 mark)**
$u = a\sqrt{x}$ for some constant value a.

$$2 = a\sqrt{9}, a = \frac{2}{3} \text{ so } u = \frac{2}{3}\sqrt{x} \qquad \textbf{(1 mark)}$$
$$y = 2 \times \frac{2}{3}\sqrt{x} = \frac{4}{3}\sqrt{x},$$
$$y = \frac{4}{3} \times \sqrt{36} = 8 \qquad \textbf{(2 marks)}$$

20. $\overrightarrow{ON} = \overrightarrow{OM} + \overrightarrow{MN}$

$$\overrightarrow{OM} = \frac{2}{3}\mathbf{a} \qquad \textbf{(1 mark)}$$
$$\overrightarrow{OB} : \overrightarrow{MN} = 3:1$$

$$\overrightarrow{MN} = \frac{1}{3}\mathbf{b} \qquad \textbf{(1 mark)}$$
$$\overrightarrow{ON} = \frac{2}{3}\mathbf{a} + \frac{1}{3}\mathbf{b} = \frac{1}{3}(2\mathbf{a}+\mathbf{b}) \qquad \textbf{(2 marks)}$$

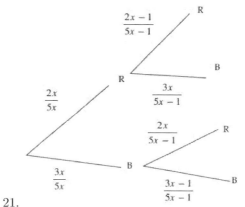

21.

Probability of getting the same colour balls

$$P(RR) + P(BB)$$

$$= \frac{2x}{5x} \times \frac{2x-1}{5x-1} + \frac{3x}{5x} \times \frac{3x-1}{5x-1} = \frac{1}{2} \qquad \textbf{(1 mark)}$$
$$\frac{2(2x-1) + 3(3x-1)}{5(5x-1)} = \frac{1}{2}$$
$$\frac{4x-2+9x-3}{25x-5} = \frac{1}{2} \qquad \textbf{(1 mark)}$$
$$\frac{13x-5}{25x-5} = \frac{1}{2}$$

$$26x - 10 = 25x - 5$$
$$26x - 25x = 10 - 5 \qquad \textbf{(2 marks)}$$
$$x = 5 \qquad \textbf{(1 mark)}$$
$5 \times 2 = 10$, reds $5 \times 3 = 15$ blue balls **(1 mark)**

SET A- Paper 2 Solutions

1. (a) 0.396964287 **(1 mark)**

   (b) 0.40 (2sf) **(1 mark)**

2. $\dfrac{43.5 - 35}{35} \times 100 = £24.29$ **(2 marks)**

3. (a)

x	-4	-3	-2	-1	0	1	2
y	-9	-3	1	3	3	1	-3

(2 marks)

   (b)

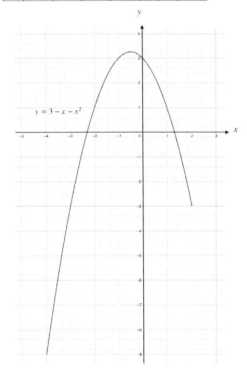

$y = 3 - x - x^2$

(2 marks)

   (c) $(0.5, 3.3) \pm 0.2$ **(1 mark)**

4. (a) 4 minutes 32 seconds $= 4 \times 60 + 32$
   $= 272$ seconds.

   $$\text{speed} = \frac{\text{distance}}{\text{time}}$$

   Therefore,
   $\dfrac{1600}{4 \times 60 + 32} = 5\dfrac{15}{17}$ (Arnav's speed) **(1 mark)**

   $1000 \div 5\dfrac{15}{17} = 170$ **(1 mark)**
   (times he takes to complete 1000 m race in minutes)

   $170 \div 60 = 2\dfrac{5}{6}, \dfrac{5}{6} \times 60 = 50$

(convert to minutes and seconds)
2 minutes 50 seconds. **(1 mark)**

   (b) He will take a shorter time to complete the race..
   (any other similar valid reasons) **(1 mark)**

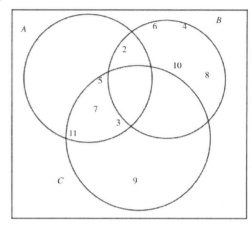

5. (a)

(3 marks)

   (b) $P(A n B') = \dfrac{4}{10} = \dfrac{2}{5}$ **(1 mark)**

6. $I\hat{J}M = L\hat{M}B = 70°$
   (Corresponding angles are equal)
   $A\hat{I}E = I\hat{L}G = 60°$ **(1 mark)**
   (Corresponding angles are equal)
   $I\hat{L}G = M\hat{L}B = 60°$ **(1 mark)**
   (Vertically opposite angles are equal)
   $M\hat{B}L = 180 - 70 - 60 = 50°$ **(1 mark)**
   (Interior angles of a triangle add to 180°)

7. Area of rectangle:
   $2.54 \times 3.5 = 8.89 \text{ m}^2$
   Area of semicircles:
   $2 \times \frac{1}{2} \times \pi \times 1.27^2 + 2 \times \frac{1}{2} \times \pi \times 1.75^2 = 14.68820\ldots \text{m}^2$

   (2 marks)

   Total area to paint:
   $14.68820\ldots + 8.89 = 23.5782\ldots \text{m}^2$ **(1 mark)**

   Amount of paint required:
   $23.5782 \div 2.4 = 9.8242\ldots \approx 10l$
   $10 \div 4 = 2.5 \approx 3$ tins **(1 mark)**

   Cost of paint:
   $3 \times 24.50 = £73.50$

   Yes, he has enough money to paint the floor.

   (1 mark)

---

8. Cash Instant Isa account:
$3000 \times 1.025^3 = 3230.67$,
$3230.67 - 3000 = £230.67$ **(2 marks)**

Flexible share account:
$3000 \times 0.035 \times 3 = £315$ **(1 mark)**

Income:
$315 - 230.67 = £84.33$

Flexible share account provides a better income.

(1 mark)

9. (a) $(2x-1)(2x-1)(x+4)$
$= (4x^2 - 4x + 1)(x+4)$ **(1 mark)**
$= 4x^3 + 16x^2 - 4x^2 - 16x + x + 4$
$= 4x^3 + 12x^2 - 15x + 4$ **(1 mark)**

(b) $2 \times \sqrt{4} \times \sqrt{2} = 2^{2n}$
$2^2 \times 2^{\frac{1}{2}} = 2^{2n}$
$2^{\frac{5}{2}} = 2^{2n}$ **(2 marks)**

$2n = \frac{5}{2}, 4n = 5, n = \frac{5}{4} = 1.25$ **(1 mark)**

10. (a) R = Event that red ball is selected
B = Event that blue ball is selected

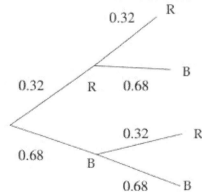

$P(\text{different colour balls}) = P(RB) + P(BR)$
$= 2 \times 0.32 \times 0.68 = 0.4352$ **(2 marks)**

(b) The events that Tina and Tim select a ball are independent. **(1 mark)**

11. The total ratio is $4 + 3 + 2 = 9$
$18 \div 9 = 2$

$2 \times 4 = 8, 2 \times 3 = 6, 2 \times 2 = 4$ **(1 mark)**

$8 \times £1.46 = £11.68, 6 \times £2.99 = £17.94$,
$\frac{1.44}{750} \times 1000 \times 4 = £7.68$ **(1 mark)**

Costs:

$£11.68 + £17.94 + £7.68 = £37.30$ **(1 mark)**

Total revenue:
$1800 \div 300 = 60, 1.08 \times 60 = £64.8$ **(1 mark)**

Profit:
$64.8 - 37.30 = £27.50$ **(1 mark)**

12. (a)

	CAR	BUS	WALK	TOTAL
MALE	150	200	200	550
FEMALE	50	150	250	450
TOTAL	200	350	450	1000

(3 marks)

(b) i. $P(\text{Male and Bus}) = \frac{200}{1000} = \frac{1}{5}$ **(1 mark)**
ii. $P(\text{Car or Walk}) = \frac{200+450}{1000} = \frac{13}{50}$ **(1 mark)**

13. $36 \div 2 = 18°$
Angle ACB is $3 \times 18 = 54°$ and angle $BAD = 90°$ **(1 mark)**

Length AB:
$\cos(36) = \frac{AB}{7}, AB = 7\cos(36)$ **(1 mark)**

Length AC:
$\sin(36) = \frac{AC}{7}, AC = 7\sin(36)$ **(1 mark)**
Area of triangle ABC:
$= \frac{1}{2} \times AC \times AB$
$= \frac{1}{2} \times 7\sin(36) \times 7\cos(36)$
$= 11.65044\ldots$
$\approx 11.7 \text{ cm}^2$ (1dp) **(1 mark)**

Alternative method
$36 \div 2 = 18°$
Angle ACB is $3 \times 18 = 54°$ and angle $BAD = 90°$

(1 mark)

Using the sine rule, $\dfrac{AB}{\sin(54)} = \dfrac{7}{\sin(90)}$

$AB = \dfrac{7}{\sin(90)} \times \sin(54)$
$= 5.66311\ldots \approx 5.663$ **(1 mark)**

Therefore, area of the triangle
$= \frac{1}{2} \times BC \times BA \times \sin(36)$
$= \frac{1}{2} \times 7 \times 5.663.. \times \sin(36)$
$= 11.65\ldots \approx 11.7\,\text{cm}^2$ **(2 marks)**

14. Let $2m+1$ and $2n+1$ be any two odd numbers and m and n be two positive integers. Then,

$(2m+1)(2n+1)$
$= 4mn + 2m + 2n + 1$

$= 2(2mn + m + n) + 1$
$(2mn + m + n)$ is an integer. **(2 marks)**

Therefore, $2(2mm + m + n)$ is an even integer, and adding one makes the expression an odd number.

Hence, multiplying any two odd numbers produces an odd number result. **(1 marks)**

15. $y = 5 - 2x, x^2 + 2(5 - 2x)^2 = 14$ **(1 mark)**

$x^2 + 2\left(4x^2 - 20x + 25\right) = 14$

$x^2 + 8x^2 - 40x + 50 = 14, 9x^2 - 40x + 36 = 0$ **(1 mark)**

$x = \dfrac{-(-40) \pm \sqrt{(-40)^2 - 4(9)(36)}}{2 \times 9}$

$= \dfrac{20 \pm 2\sqrt{19}}{9}$ **(1 mark)**

$x = \dfrac{20 + 2\sqrt{19}}{9} = 3.190866\ldots \approx 3.19(3sf)$

$y = 5 + 2\left(\dfrac{20 - 2\sqrt{19}}{9}\right)$

$= -1.3817\ldots \approx -1.38(3sf)$ **(1 mark)**

When,
$x = \dfrac{20 - 2\sqrt{19}}{9} = 1.25357\ldots \approx 1.25(3sf),$

$y = 5 - 2\left(\dfrac{20 - 2\sqrt{19}}{9}\right)$

$= 2.4928\ldots \approx 2.49(3sf)$ **(1 mark)**

16.

	Lower bound	Upper bound
a	9.75	9.85
s	3.245	3.255
v	-8.15	-8.25

(3 marks)

$u^2 = v^2 - 2as$

$u = \sqrt{v^2 - 2as}$

Lower bound of u:

$u = \sqrt{(-8.15)^2 - 2(9.85)(3.255)}$

$= 1.516245\ldots \approx 1.52(2sf)$ **(1 mark)**

Upper bound of u:

$u = \sqrt{(-8.25)^2 - 2(1.75)(3.245)}$
$= 2.18746\ldots \approx 2.19(3sf)$ **(1 mark)**

17.
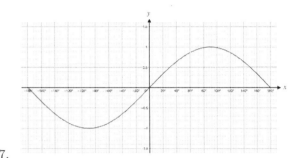

(2 marks)

18. $\dfrac{1}{x - 1} + \dfrac{x(2x + 1)}{x - 1} \times \dfrac{(x + 1)(x - 1)}{2x(2x + 1)}$ **(2 marks)**

$\dfrac{1}{x - 1} + \dfrac{\cancel{x}\cancel{(2x + 1)}}{\cancel{(x - 1)}} \times \dfrac{(x + 1)\cancel{(x - 1)}}{2\cancel{x}\cancel{(2x + 1)}}$

$= \dfrac{1}{x - 1} + \dfrac{x + 1}{2}$ **(1 mark)**

$\dfrac{2 + (x - 1)(x + 1)}{2(x - 1)} = \dfrac{2 + x^2 - 1}{2(x - 1)}$

$= \dfrac{x^2 + 1}{2(x - 1)}$ **(2 marks)**

19. $2 = ab^0, a = 2$ **(1 mark)**

$8 = ab^2, 8 = 2b^2,$
$b^2 = 4 \quad b = \pm 2, b = 2$ **(1 mark)**

20. $B\hat{O}D = 180° - B\hat{A}D = 180 - x$
(Opposite angles of cyclic quadrilateral add to 180°) **(2 marks)**

$B\hat{C}D = \frac{1}{2}B\hat{O}D = \frac{180 - x}{2} = 90 - \frac{1}{2}x$
(Angle in circumference is half the angle at the center.) **(2 marks)**

SET A – Paper 3 Solutions

1. $13.4 \text{ cm} \leq x < 13.5 \text{ cm}$ **(2 marks)**

2. The total ratio is $2 + 3 = 5$.

   Each part of the ratio is equivalent to $10 \div 5 = 2$ kg.

   $2 \times 2 = 4$ kg of tomatoes are used for making tomato paste. $3 \times 2 = 6$ kg of tomatoes are used for making tomato puree.

                                            (1 mark)

   $4 \times 2 \times £1.50 = £12$ is received from sales of 8 cans of tomato paste.

   $6 \times 2 \times £2 = £24$ is received from sales of 12 cans of tomato puree.   **(1 mark)**

   Hence, the total revenue is $24 + 12 = £36$.

   Therefore, the percentage profit $= \frac{36-20}{20} \times 100\% = 80\%$.

                                            (1 mark)

3. (a) The cost of sending the small letter is

   $$14 \times 2.25 + 8 \times 2.34 = £50.22$$

   The cost of sending the large letter is

   $$2.36 \times 5 + 9 \times 2.93 + 3 \times 3.39 = £48.34$$

   Hence, the total cost of sending the letter is

   $50.22 + 48.34 = £98.56$ **(2 marks)**

   (b) The cost of sending the parcel under $1\,kg$ is

   $7 \times 4.20 + 9 \times 6.30 = £86.10$

   The cost of sending the remaining parcels using the first-class stamp is

   $4 \times 4.85 + 3 \times 10.02 = £56.34$

   So, the total cost is

   $86.10 + 56.34 = £142.44$ **(2 marks)**

   (c) The total cost of sending the parcel and letter

   $= 98.56 + 142.44 = £241$

   However,

   the total cost of sending the letters using the second-class stamp is

   $14 \times 2.06 + 8 \times 2.17 + 5 \times 2.36 + 9 \times 2.93 + 3 \times 3.39$
   $= £94.54$

The total cost of sending the parcel using the second-class stamp is

$(7 + 4) \times 4.22 + (9 + 3) \times 6.30 = £121.8$

Therefore, the total cost of sending all the letters and parcels by second-class stamp

$= 121.8 + 94.54 = £216.34$ **(2 marks)**

The total saving

$= 241 - 216.34 = £24.66$ **(1 mark)**

4. The single transformation that maps shape A to shape C is a rotation of $180°$ clockwise or anti clockwise about the point $(4, 2)$.   **(2 marks)**

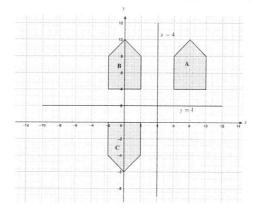

                                         (1 mark)

Alternative method:

The single transformation that maps shape A to shape C could also be an enlargement by scale factor -1 about the point $(4, 2)$.   **(3 marks)**

5. $28 \div 7 = 4$ (one part of the ratio represents 4 staff.) Hence,
there are $10 \times 4 = 40$ operation staff. **(1 mark)**
$40 \div 5 = 8$ (now, one part of the ratio represents 8 staffs)
Therefore, there are $8 \times 8 = 64$ sales staff. **(2 marks)**
Alternative method:
Let:
x be the number of sales staff
y be the number of operational staff
z be the number of finance staff

Solve y using the given operation and finance staff ratio. Substitute $z = 28$.

$$\frac{y}{z} = \frac{10}{7}$$
$$\frac{y}{28} = \frac{10}{7}$$
$$y = 40$$ **(1 mark)**

Solve x using the given sales staff and operation staff ratio. Substitute $y = 40$.

$$\frac{x}{y} = \frac{8}{5}$$
$$\frac{x}{40} = \frac{8}{5}$$
$$x = 64 \qquad \textbf{(2 marks)}$$

Therefore, there are 64 sales staff in the company.

6. The LCM of a and b is the smallest multiple that is divisible by both a and b.
Let $a = 6$ and $b = 8$.
Prime factorisation of 6: 2×3
Prime factorisation of 8: $2 \times 2 \times 2$ **(1 mark)**
The LCM of 6 and 8 is
$2 \times 2 \times 2 \times 3 = 24$ **(1 mark)**

Similarly, the LCM of 10^{12} and 10^{22} is
$10^{12} \times 10^{10} = 10^{22}$
Therefore, the LCM of 6×10^{12} and 8×10^{22}
is 24×10^{22} or 2.4×10^{23} **(1 mark)**

7. (a) Positive correlation.   **(1 mark)**

(b) As the number of breaths per minute increases, the number of heartbeats per minute also increases.

    (1 mark)

(c) The gradient of the line of best fit shows the rate of increase in heartbeats per minute for an increase in breaths per minute.   **(1 mark)**

8. $density(d) = \frac{mass(m)}{volume(v)}$
$d = \frac{5}{20} = 0.25 kg/cm^3$
is the original density of the object.
The mass increases by 20% and the volume decreases by 50%.
So, the percentage multiplier for the mass is
$100 + 20 = 120\% = 1.2$,
and for the volume it is
$100 - 50 = 50\% = 0.5$
Hence,
$d = \frac{1.2 \times 5}{0.5 \times 20}$ **(1 mark)**

$d = \frac{1.2}{0.5} \times \frac{5}{20}$

$d = 2.4 \times 0.25$ **(1 mark)**
Hence, the percentage multiplier of the original density is $2.4 \times 100 = 240\%$. This is an increase of $240 - 100 = 140\%$ on the original density of the

object.

    (1 mark)

Alternative method: Use the formula of density,
$d = \frac{m}{v}$ where:
d is the density
m is the mass
v is the volume

Solve for the initial density.

$$d = \frac{m}{v}$$
$$= \frac{5{,}000\,\text{g}}{120\,\text{cm}^3}$$
$$= 41.67\,\text{g/cm}^3 \qquad \textbf{(1 mark)}$$

Find the new mass and volume:

Mass is increased by 20%: $5{,}000 \times 1.20 = 6{,}000$
Volume is decreased by 50%: $120 \div 2 = 60$
Find the new density:

$$d = \frac{m}{v}$$
$$= \frac{6{,}000\,\text{g}}{60\,\text{cm}^3}$$
$$= 100\,\text{g/cm}^3 \qquad \textbf{(1 mark)}$$

Find the percentage change of density:

$$\%\Delta\text{density} = \frac{100 - 41.67}{41.67} \times 100\%$$
$$\approx 140\%$$

Therefore, density is increased by 140%. **(1 mark)**

9. (a) $-10, -25, -36$ **(1 mark)**

(b) $2n^2 - 21n + 9 = 6n - 4$
$2n^2 - 27n + 13 = 0$
$(2n - 1)(n - 13) = 0$ **(1 mark)**
Therefore, $n = \frac{1}{2}$ or $n = 13$
However, n must be an integer. So, both sequences have the same 13th term.
Therefore, the term is
$6 \times 12 - 4 = 74$.   **(1 mark)**

10. Find the measure of each angle.
Let x be the ratio multiplier, then the total angles in the triangle add up to $180°$

$$x + 2x + 3x = 180°$$
$$6x = 180°$$
$$x = 30°$$
$$2x = 60°$$
$$3x = 90° \qquad \textbf{(1 mark)}$$

Notice that the triangle is a right-angled triangle with $90°$ being the largest angle.

Let x be the measurement of the smallest side. Let y be the measurement of the longer side. Then $2 : \sqrt{3} = 25 : y$ so,

$$\frac{\sqrt{3}}{2} = \frac{y}{25}$$
$$y = \frac{25 \times \sqrt{3}}{2}$$
$$y = 12.5\sqrt{3}$$

$$\frac{1}{\sqrt{3}} = \frac{x}{y}$$
$$x = \frac{1 \times 12.5\sqrt{3}}{\sqrt{3}}$$
$$x = 12.5 \qquad \textbf{(2 marks)}$$

To illustrate the triangle:

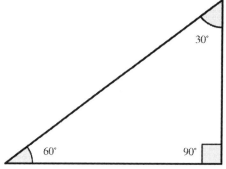

Calculate the area using the formula $A = \dfrac{b \times h}{2}$.

$$A = \frac{12.5 \times 12.5\sqrt{3}}{2}$$
$$= \frac{625\sqrt{2}}{8} \text{ cm}^2 \qquad \textbf{(1 mark)}$$

11. (a) Two x terms that multiply to give x^2 are x and x. Two numbers that multiply to give $+3$ and multiply to give -4 are -1 and -2.
Therefore, the quadratic expression factorises to give
$$(x-1)(x-3)$$

(1 mark)

(b) Apply the difference between two identities to the expression.

$$\big[(4\pi + 1) - (4\pi - 1)\big]\big[(4\pi + 1) + (4\pi - 1)\big]$$
$$= (4\pi + 1 - 4\pi + 1)(4\pi + 1 + 4\pi - 1)$$
$$= (2)(8\pi) = 16\pi \qquad \textbf{(3 marks)}$$

Alternative method:
Expand the bracket $(4\pi + 1)^2$ to give

$$(4\pi + 1)^2 = (4\pi)^2 + 2 \times 4\pi \times 1 + 1^2$$
$$= 16\pi^2 + 8\pi + 1 \qquad \textbf{(1 mark)}$$

Expand the bracket $(4\pi - 1)^2$ to give

$$(4\pi - 1)^2 = (4\pi)^2 - 2 \times 4\pi \times 1 + 1^2$$
$$= 16\pi^2 - 8\pi + 1 \qquad \textbf{(1 mark)}$$

Simplify
$$(4\pi + 1)^2 - (4\pi - 1)^2$$
$$= 16\pi^2 + 8\pi + 1 - \big(16\pi^2 - 8\pi + 1\big)$$
$$= 16\pi^2 + 8\pi + 1 - 16\pi^2 + 8\pi - 1$$
$$= 16\pi \qquad \textbf{(1 mark)}$$

12. (a) $100\% - 12\% = 88\% = 0.88$, $p_{t+1} = 0.88p_t$

(2 marks)

(b)

Year	Start of the year	End of the year
1	2,000	$2,000 \times 0.88 = 17.60$
2	200×0.88	$200 \times 0.88^2 = 1,548.80$
3	200×0.88^2	$200 \times 0.88^3 = 1,362.9 \approx 1362$

(3 marks)

13. (a) The equation of a straight line with gradient m and intercept c on the y-axis is

$$y = mx + c \qquad \textbf{(1 mark)}$$

Find m using the formula

$$m = \frac{y_2 - y_1}{x_2 - x_1}$$

The line passes through the points $(2, 2)$ and $(6, 4)$. Therefore, the gradient of the line is

$$m = \frac{4 - 2}{6 - 2}$$
$$m = \frac{1}{2} \qquad \textbf{(1 mark)}$$

Hence, the equation of the line is

$$y = \frac{1}{2}x + c$$

Substitute one of the two co-ordinates into the equation to find the y intercept.
Using the co-ordinate $(2,2)$ in the equation, we get

$$2 = \frac{1}{2} \times (2) + c$$
$$2 = 1 + c$$
$$c = 1$$

Now, substitute the value of m and c.

$$y = \frac{1}{2}x + 1 \qquad \textbf{(1 mark)}$$

(b) The gradient of two perpendicular lines are negative reciprocals of each other. Therefore, the gradient of the line perpendicular to line l is -2. Solve for y intercept c by substituting $x = -2$ and $y = 6$. **(1 mark)**

$$y = -2x + c$$
$$6 = -2(-2) + c$$
$$c = 2 \qquad \textbf{(1 mark)}$$

Therefore,

$$y = -2x + 2 \qquad \textbf{(1 mark)}$$

14. (a)

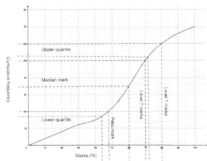

Find the halfway point from the top of the graph.

$$\frac{1}{2}(70) = 35$$

From the graph, the median mark is 60% when the cumulative frequency is 35. **(1 mark)**

(b) The lower quartile is $\frac{1}{4}$ from the top of the graph.

$$\frac{1}{4}(70) = 17.5$$

Hence, from the graph, the lower quartile is 44%. The upper quartile is $\frac{3}{4}$ from the top of the graph.

$$\frac{3}{4}(70) = 52.5$$

Hence, the upper quartile is 72% from the graph. The interquartile range is the difference between the upper and lower quartiles.

$$72\% - 44\% = 28\%$$

Thus, the interquartile range is 28%. **(2 marks)**

(c) From the graph, the students that have marks greater than or equal to 48% fall on the range of 70 and 20.

$$70 - 20 = 50 \text{ students} \qquad \textbf{(1 mark)}$$

(d) From the graph, the students that have marks of 70%–80% fall on the range of 50 to 60.

$$60 - 50 = 10 \text{ students} \qquad \textbf{(1 mark)}$$

$$\frac{10}{70} \times 100\% = 14.29\% \qquad \textbf{(1 mark)}$$

15. Factorise 3 from the first two terms.

$$3(x^2 - 4x) + 13$$

Complete the square.

$$3[(x - 2)^2 - 2^2] + 13$$
$$2(x - 2)^2 - 8 + 13$$
$$2(x - 2)^2 + 5$$

So, $a = 2$, $b = 2$ and $c = 5$ **(3 marks)**

16. (a) The height of the cone $= 5 - 1 = 4$ cm
The radius of the cone $= x - 1 = 5 - 1 = 4 \, cm$

(1 mark)

The volume V of the cone is given by the formula

$$V = \frac{1}{3}\pi r^2 h$$

Hence, substitute $h = 4$ and $r = 4$ to find the volume.

$$V = \frac{1}{3} \times 4^2 \times 4$$
$$= \frac{64\pi}{3} \, cm^3$$

(1 mark

(b) The area of the circle $= \pi r^2 = \pi \times 4^2 = 16\pi$

The area of the curved surface is given by the formula

$$A = \pi r l$$

where r is the radius and l is the slanted height of the cone.

$$l^2 = r^2 + h^2$$
$$l = \sqrt{4^2 + 4^2} = \sqrt{32} = 4\sqrt{2}$$

(2 marks)

Therefore, the curved surface area is

$$= \pi \times 4 \times 4\sqrt{2} = 16\sqrt{2}\pi$$

Hence, the total surface is of the cone is

$$16\pi + 16\sqrt{2}\pi = 16\pi(1 + \sqrt{2})$$

(2 marks)

17. From the diagram $OA = OB = OD = 4cm$.
They are the radius of the same circle.
The triangle ABC is an isosceles triangle and angle $BAO = ABO = 75°$.
The angle $AOB = 180 - 75 - 75 = 30°$ as the angles in the triangle AOB add up to $180°$.
The angle $AOB = OBC = 30°$ as alternate angles are equal angles.
The angle $BCD = 90°$ since the angles in a semicircle are always $90°$.

(2 marks)

Using the triangle BCD,

$$\sin(30) = \frac{CD}{BD}$$

Hence,

$$CD = BD \times \sin(30) = 8 \times \frac{1}{2} = 4\,cm$$

(1 mark)

and

$$\cos(30) = \frac{BC}{BD}$$
$$BC = BD \times \cos(30) = 8 \times \frac{\sqrt{3}}{2} = 4\sqrt{3}cm$$

(1 mark)

The area of triangle BCD

$$= \frac{hb}{2} = \frac{4 \times 4\sqrt{3}}{2} = 8\sqrt{3}$$

(1 mark)

Time in minutes	Frequency	Class interval	Frequency density
$0 < t \leq 6$	3	6	$3 \div 6 = 0.5$
$6 < t \leq 10$	8	4	$8 \div 4 = 2$
$10 < t \leq 12$	5	2	$5 \div 2 = 2.5$
$12 < t \leq 15$	**12**	3	$12 \div 3 = 4$
$15 < t \leq 20$	3	5	$3 \div 5 = 0.6$

18. (a)

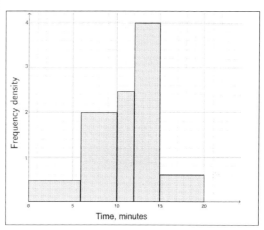

(2 marks)

(b)

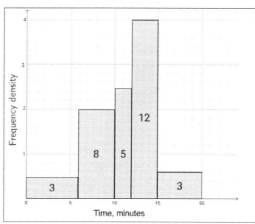

The total frequency is

$$3 + 8 + 5 + 12 + 3 = 31$$

The median is the mid value of the distribution. Hence,

$$\frac{31}{2} = 15.5$$

15.5 lies on the class interval $10 < t \leq 12$. Add the first two frequencies to give

$$3 + 8 = 11$$

To reach 15.5, we need to find $\frac{15.5-11}{5} \times 2 = 1.8$
Add the time of the first two frequencies

$$6 + 4 = 10$$

So, the median is

$$10 + 1.8 = 11.8 \text{ minutes} \qquad \textbf{(2 marks)}$$

(c) The number of people who took between $11 < t \leq 12$ minutes is $\frac{1}{2}$ of the number of people who took between $10 < t \leq 12$ minutes. The number of people who took between $12 < t \leq 13$ minutes is $\frac{1}{3}$ of the number of people who took between $12 < t \leq 15$ minutes. Therefore, the number of people who took between 11 and 13 minutes is

$$\frac{1}{2} \times 5 + \frac{1}{3} \times 12 = 6.5$$

Hence,

$$\frac{6.5}{31} \times 100 = 20.97 \approx 21.0\%$$

$$\textbf{(2 marks)}$$

19. When the value of the investment increases by $x\%$ in the first year, the percentage multiplier is

$$\frac{100 + x}{100}$$

When the value increases by $\frac{1}{4}x$ in the second year, the percentage multiplier is

$$\frac{100 + 0.25x}{100}$$

Hence,

$$£7,500 \times \left(\frac{100 + x}{100}\right) \times \left(\frac{100 + 0.25x}{100}\right) = £8,456.25$$

$$\textbf{(2 marks)}$$

$$£7,500 \times \left(\frac{(100 + x)(100 + 0.25)}{100 \times 100}\right) = £8,456.25$$
$$£75 \times (100 + x)(100 + 0.25x) = £8,456.25 \times 100$$
$$(100 + x)(100 + 0.25x) = 11,275$$
$$10,000 + 125x + 0.25x^2 - 11,275 = 11,275 - 11,275$$
$$0.25x^2 + 125x - 1,275 = 0 \qquad \textbf{(2 marks)}$$

$$x_{1,2} = \frac{-125 \pm \sqrt{125^2 - 4 \times 0.25\,(-1275)}}{2 \times 0.25}$$
$$x_1 = \frac{-125 + 130}{2 \times 0.25}, \; x_2 = \frac{-125 - 130}{2 \times 0.25}$$
$$x_1 = 10, \; x_2 = -510$$
$$x > 0 \text{ so } x = 10$$

$$\textbf{(2 marks)}$$

SET B -Paper 1 Solutions

1. (a) The given fractions are $\frac{1}{2}, \frac{4}{5}, \frac{2}{3}$
   which is equal to: $\frac{15}{30}, \frac{24}{30}, \frac{20}{30}$ **(1 mark)**

   Since $\frac{15}{30} \le \frac{20}{30} \le \frac{24}{30}$

   the increasing order is $\frac{1}{2}, \frac{2}{3}, \frac{4}{5}$. **(1 mark)**

   (b) Here,
   $$\frac{7^{10} \times 7^{-4}}{7^4} = 7^{10 + \{-4\} - 4} \quad \textbf{(1 mark)}$$
   $$= 7^2$$
   $$= 49 \quad \textbf{(1 mark)}$$

2. The selling price of 10 T-shirts
   $$= £108 + 0.10(108)$$
   $$= £118.80 \quad \textbf{(1 mark)}$$
   Now John has only $12 - 2 = 10$ T-shirts,
   so the selling price of 1 T-shirt is:
   $$= \frac{£118.80}{10}$$
   $$= £11.88 \quad \textbf{(1 mark)}$$

3. The difference between the ratio of the present ages and 2 years later is 1.
   This means 1 part of the ratio is equivalent to 2 years.

   (1mark)

   Therefore their present ages are
   $2 \times 7 = 14$ and $2 \times 4 = 8$. **(2 mark)**
   Alternative method:
   Let their ages be x and y years.
   $$\frac{x}{y} = \frac{7}{4}$$
   Then, $$4x = 7y$$
   $$4x - 7y = 0 \dots\dots\dots\dots\dots(1) \quad \textbf{(1 mark)}$$

   Also,
   $$\frac{x+2}{y+2} = \frac{8}{5}$$
   $$5x + 10 = 8y + 16$$
   $5x - 8y - 6 = 0 \dots\dots\dots\dots(2)$ **(1 mark)**
   Solving (1) and (2) we get
   $x = 14$ and $y = 8$
   So, their present ages are 14 and 8 years. **(1 mark)**

4. (a) It takes 6 days to finish if there are 20 people.
   It takes 1 day to finish if there are 20×6 people. **(1 mark)**

   It takes 2 days to finish if there are
   $\frac{20 \times 6}{2} = 60$ people. **(1 mark)**

   (b) Here, 20 people can finish the project in 6 days.
   1 person can finish the project in 6×20 days. **(1 mark)**

   15 people can finish the project in
   $\frac{6 \times 20}{15} = 8$ days.
   (1 mark)

   (c) All people work at the same rate. **(1 mark)**

5. (a) Completed table

x	-2	-1	0	1	2	3	4
y	4	-1	-4	-5	-4	-1	4

   (2 marks)

   (b)

   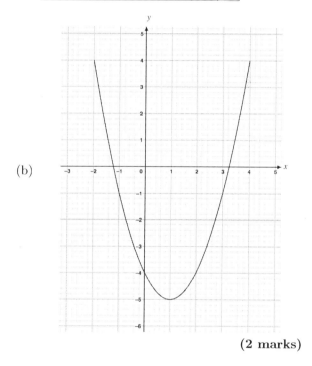

   (2 marks)

   (c) The curve $y = x^2 - 2x - 4$ meets the x-axis at -1.2 and 3.2.
   So the solutions for $x^2 - 2x - 4 = 0$ are
   $x = -1.2, 3.2$. **(1 mark)**
   Allow solutions in the range -1.1 to -1.3 and 3.1 to 3.3.

6. (a) The cost of 1 kg chicken is C and the cost of 1 kg mutton is M. So the pair of linear equations is
   $$3C + M = 11 \quad (1)$$
   $$2C + 3M = 19 \quad (2)$$
   (2 marks)

(b) Multiplying (1) by 3 and subtracting (2) from (1) we get,

$$7C = 14$$
$$C = 2 \qquad \textbf{(1 mark)}$$

Substituting $C = 2$ into (1),

$$3(2) + M = 11$$
$$M = 5 \qquad \textbf{(1 mark)}$$

So, the price of 1 kg chicken is £2 and the price of 1 kg mutton is £5. **(1 mark)**

7. The first reflection is in $x = -1$. **(1 mark)**
The second reflection is in $y = 2$. **(1 mark)**
The single transformation is a 180° rotation about the point$(-1, 2)$.
Or, enlargement by scale factor -1 from the point $(-1, 2)$. **(2 marks)**

8. Let the original production cost of the item be x, and the original weight of the item be y.
Since the production cost increased by 20%, the new cost is 100% of $x + 20\%$ of $x = 1.2x$ for weight y. However, if you need to keep the production cost down to the original price x we need to reduce the weight of the item to $\dfrac{y}{1.2}$. **(1 mark)**
Therefore the decrease in weight is

$$y - \frac{y}{1.2} = \frac{0.2y}{1.2} \qquad \textbf{(1 mark)}$$

The percentage decrease in weight is:

$$= \frac{\frac{0.2y}{1.2}}{y} \times 100\%$$
$$= \frac{100}{6}\%$$
$$= 16\frac{2}{3}\% \qquad \textbf{(1 mark)}$$

9. (a) The frequency for the number of 3-year-old children is highest, so the modal age is 3. **(1 mark)**

(b) The total frequency (N) is 19.

$$\text{median} = \left(\frac{N+1}{2}\right)^{\text{th}} \text{term}$$
$$= (\frac{20}{2})^{\text{th}} \text{term}$$
$$= 10^{\text{th}} \text{term}$$

So, the median is 5. **(2 mark)**

10. (a)

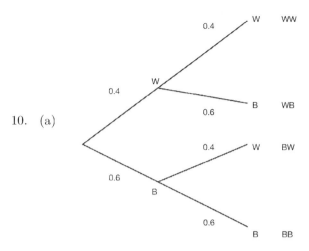

Probability of same colour:
$$= P(WW) + P(BB)$$
$$= 0.4 \times 0.4 + 0.6 \times 0.6$$
$$= 0.52 \qquad \textbf{(3 marks)}$$

(b) $0.6 \times 40 = 24$ **(1 mark)**

11. (a) The relationship between $\mathbf{a}$ and $\mathbf{b}$ is:

$$\mathbf{b} = \begin{pmatrix} 9 \\ 6 \end{pmatrix}$$
$$\mathbf{b} = 3\begin{pmatrix} 3 \\ 2 \end{pmatrix}$$
$$\mathbf{b} = 3\mathbf{a}$$

So, $\mathbf{a}$ and $\mathbf{b}$ are parallel. **(1 mark)**

(b) The sum of $\mathbf{a} + \mathbf{b}$ is:

$$\mathbf{a} + \mathbf{b} = \begin{pmatrix} 12 \\ 8 \end{pmatrix} \qquad \textbf{(1 mark)}$$

The magnitude of $\mathbf{a} + \mathbf{b}$
$$= \sqrt{12^2 + 8^2}$$
$$= 4\sqrt{13} \qquad \textbf{(2 marks)}$$

12. (a)
$$\frac{1}{a+b} + \frac{b}{a^2 - b^2}$$
$$= \frac{1}{a+b} + \frac{b}{(a+b)(a-b)} \qquad \textbf{(1 mark)}$$
$$= \frac{a - b + b}{a^2 - b^2}$$
$$= \frac{a}{a^2 - b^2} \qquad \textbf{(1 mark)}$$

(b) $45 - 9p^2$
$$= 5(9 - p^4)$$
$$= 5[(3)^2 - (p^2)^2] \qquad \textbf{(1 mark)}$$
$$= 5(3 + p^2)(3 - p^2) \qquad \textbf{(1 mark)}$$

13. (a) The area of triangle $ABC = \frac{1}{2}AC \times AB$.
Since $AC = AB$,

$$\text{area} = \frac{1}{2}AB^2$$

$$\frac{1}{2}AB^2 = 18 \qquad \textbf{(1 mark)}$$

$$AB^2 = 36$$

$$AB = 6 \text{ cm} \qquad \textbf{(1 mark)}$$

Using the Pythagorean theorem,

$$BC = \sqrt{6^2 + 6^2} = 6\sqrt{2} \qquad \textbf{(1 mark)}$$

So the perimeter P is:

$$P = 6 + 6 + 6\sqrt{2}$$

$$= 12 + 6\sqrt{2} \text{ cm} \qquad \textbf{(1 mark)}$$

(b) The value of $\cos 60° = \dfrac{1}{2}$ **(1 mark)**

14. Let m be any even number. Then,
    $m = 2n$ for some integer n **(1 mark)**
    Then,
    $$m^2 = (2n)^2$$
    $$= 4n^2 = 4(n^2)$$

    So m^2 is multiple of 4.
    Hence, the square of any even number
    is divisible by 4.   **(2 marks)**

15. Here,
    $$\sqrt{3}(\sqrt{18} + \sqrt{50}) = m\sqrt{6}$$
    $$\sqrt{3}(3\sqrt{2} + 5\sqrt{2}) = m\sqrt{6} \qquad \textbf{(1 mark)}$$
    $$\sqrt{3}(8\sqrt{2}) = m\sqrt{6} \qquad \textbf{(1 mark)}$$
    $$8\sqrt{6} = m\sqrt{6}$$
    $$m = 8 \qquad \textbf{(1 mark)}$$

16. Here,
    $$a = b^x$$
    $$a = (c^y)^x$$
    $$a = (a^z)^{yx} \qquad \textbf{(1 mark)}$$
    $$a = a^{xyz} \qquad \textbf{(1 mark)}$$

    So, $xyz = 1$ **(1 mark)**

17. Here,
    $$-4 \geq \frac{10 - 2n}{5} \geq -6; \quad \frac{n}{3} + 2 > 8$$
    $$-20 \geq 10 - 2n \geq -30; \quad \frac{n}{3} > 6 \qquad \textbf{(1 mark)}$$
    $$-30 \geq -2n \geq -40; \quad n > 18 \qquad \textbf{(1 mark)}$$
    $$30 \leq 2n \leq 40; \quad n > 18 \qquad \textbf{(1 mark)}$$
    $$15 \leq n \leq 20; \quad n > 18 \qquad \textbf{(1 mark)}$$
    So, $n = 19, 20$ **(1 mark)**

18. (a) Let

$$x = 2.5\dot{7}\dot{6} - - - - - - - (1)$$
$$100x = 2576.\dot{5}7\dot{6} - - - - - (II) \qquad \textbf{(1 mark)}$$

Subtracting (1) from (2) we get

$$999x = 2574$$
$$x = \frac{2574}{999} \qquad \textbf{(1 mark)}$$
$$= \frac{286}{111} \qquad \textbf{(1 mark)}$$

(b)
$$4x^2 - 7x = -3$$
$$x^2 - \frac{7x}{4} = -\frac{3}{4}$$
$$\left(x - \frac{7}{8}\right)^2 - \left(\frac{7}{8}\right)^2 = -\frac{3}{4} \qquad \textbf{(1 mark)}$$
$$\left(x - \frac{7}{8}\right)^2 = -\frac{3}{4} + \left(\frac{7}{8}\right)^2$$
$$\left(x - \frac{7}{8}\right)^2 = \frac{1}{64}$$
$$x - \frac{7}{8} = \pm\sqrt{\frac{1}{64}} = \pm\frac{1}{8} \qquad \textbf{(1 mark)}$$
$$x = \frac{7}{8} \pm \frac{1}{8}$$
$$x = \frac{7}{8} + \frac{1}{8} = 1$$
or
$$x = \frac{7}{8} - \frac{1}{8} = \frac{6}{8} = \frac{3}{4}$$
    (1 mark)

19. Here, $A\hat{B}C = 90°$.(Angle in semi circle is 90°.)
    Then,
    $$2x + 90° + 3x = 180° \qquad \textbf{(1 mark)}$$
    $$5x = 90°$$
    $$x = 18° \qquad \textbf{(1 mark)}$$

    The angle standing on the same arc are equal angles.
    Therefore,
    $$C\hat{D}B = C\hat{A}B$$
    $$= 2x$$
    $$= 2 \times 18°$$
    $$= 36° \qquad \textbf{(2 marks)}$$

20. (a) Upper quartile = Interquartile range+Lower quartile

$$= 5.5 + 8.5 = 14.$$

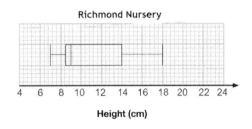

Richmond Nursery

Height (cm)

(3 marks)

(b) Petunia Nursery and Richmond Nursery have the same median value.

However, the lower and upper quartiles for the Richmond Nursery are higher, which suggests that the heights of the plants at Richmond Nursery are greater than those at Petunia Nursery.

(2 marks)

SET B- Paper 2 Solutions

1. $0.61860... = 0.619$ (3 dp) **(1 mark)**

2. (a) $6x - 4 = 4x - 8$
   $6x - 4x = -8 + 4$ **(1 mark)**
   $2x = -4$
   $x = -2$ **(1 mark)**

   (b) $3x - (x - 3)^2 = 3x - (x^2 - 6x + 9)$ **(1 mark)**
   $= 3x - x^2 + 6x - 9$
   $= 9x - x^2 - 9 = -x^2 + 9x - 9$ **(1 mark)**

3. Total distributed amount
   $= 75\%$ of £160$= $£120

   (1 mark)

   Now, the amount son received is as follows
   $= \frac{2}{5}$of $120 = \frac{2 \times 120}{2+3}$
   $= \frac{240}{5}$
   $= $£48 **(1 mark)**

4. Dina is incorrect.
   For the first digit, we can choose any of these:
   $5, 6, 7, 8, 9$
   Given that the sum of the first two-digit is 14, we have only one choice for the second digit.
   We can choose any of these for the third digit:
   $0, 2, 4, 6, 8$.

   (1 mark)

   Therefore, the total number of choices $= 5 \times 1 \times 5 = 25$

   (1 mark)

5. Offer 1:

   $$420 \times 0.8 \times 1.15 = £386.4$$

   (2 marks)

   Offer 2:

   $$420 \times 1.1 \times 0.35 = £392.7$$

   Thus, offer 1 gives him the best value for the money.

   (2 marks)

   Alternative method:
   for offer 1,
   Amount after the discount $= 420 - 20\%$ of 420
   $= 420 - 84$
   $= $£336 **(1 mark)**
   Amount with the inclusion of tax $= 336 + 15\%$ of 336

   $= 336 + 50.40$
   $= $£386.40 **(1 mark)**
   for offer 2,
   Amount with the inclusion of tax $= 420 + 10\%$ of 420
   $= 420 + 42$
   $= $£462 **(1 mark)**
   Amount after the inclusion of discount $= 462 - 15\%$ of 462
   $= 462 - 69.3$
   $= $£392.7 Given that offer 1 gives him better value for money, he should choose to offer 1. **(1 mark)**

6. (a) Since $42 = 2 \times 3 \times 7$
   and $18 = 2 \times 3 \times 3$ **(1 mark)**

   The greatest number of students James can distribute is the HCF of 42 and 18.
   $= 2 \times 3 = 6$ **(1 mark)**

   (b) The smallest number of pens and pencils David needs to buy is the LCM of 42 and 18.
   $= 2 \times 3 \times 7 \times 3$
   $= 126$ **(1 mark)**
   Thus, pack of pencils $= \frac{126}{18} = 7$
   and pack of pens $= \frac{126}{42} = 3$ **(1 mark)**

7. (a) This forms the arithmetic sequence. The nth term of the arithmetic sequence is

   $$5n + 16$$

   (1 mark)
   So,
   $16 + 5n = 166$
   $5n = 166 - 16$
   $n = \frac{150}{5}$
   $n = 30$ **(1 mark)**

   (b) No.
   The number of tickets he is collecting each month is five. He had 16 tickets at the beginning.
   Since $297 - 16 = 281$ and it is not divisible by 5, Albert can't have 297 tickets.

   (1 mark)

8. (a) Diameter (d) of the tyre $= 70\,cm$
   Thus, the exact circumference $= \pi d = 70\pi\,cm$

   (1 mark)

   (b) The total distance is as follows:$= 11\,km$
   $= 11000\,m$
   Circumference of the tyre: $= 70\pi\,cm$

$= \frac{70\pi}{100} = 0.7\pi \ m$ **(1 mark)**

So, the number of complete revolutions is as follows:$= \frac{11000}{0.7\pi}$

$= 5002$ **(1 mark)**

9. (a)

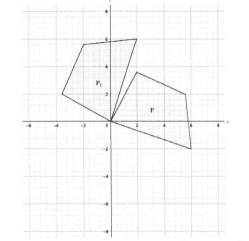

Correct rotation figure. **(2 marks)**

(b)

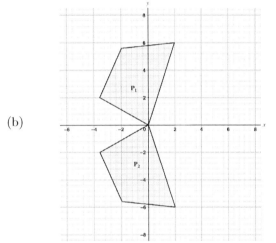

Correct reflection on the x-axis. **(2 marks)**

(c) Reflection on the line $y = -x$ gives $\mathbf{P_2}$.

(2 marks)

(d) Point $O(0,0)$ is invariant in this whole transformation as it is the only point that is not transformed.

(1 mark)

10. (a) 5 parts of the ratio = 250 students.
1 part of the ratio$= \frac{250}{5} = 50$.
4 parts $= 4 \times 50 = 200$ are boys.

(1 mark)

Therefore, the total number of students $= 250 + 200 = 450$

(1 mark)

(b) Since the teacher to student ratio is $1:25$
The total number of teachers $= \frac{450}{25} = 18$

(1 mark)

(c) Here, the mean weight $\bar{x} = 19 + 2m$
Sum of their weight $\sum x = 1330 + 140m$
Since, $\bar{x} = \frac{\sum x}{\text{total number of boys}(n)}$
Or, $19 + 2m = \frac{1330 + 140m}{n}$ **(1 mark)**
Or,$n = \frac{1330 + 140m}{19 + 2m}$
$n = \frac{70(19 + 2m)}{19 + 2m} = 70$
So, the number of boys $= 70$ **(1 mark)**

11. (a) A complete tree diagram shows all the probabilities of drawing two balls. **(3 marks)**
W= White marble is drawn.
R= Red marble is drawn.

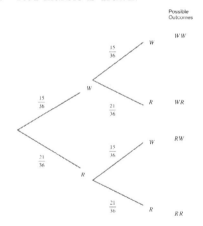

(b) From the tree diagram
$P(\text{same colour})=P(WW) + P(RR)$
$= \frac{21}{36} \times \frac{21}{36} + \frac{15}{36} \times \frac{15}{36}$
$= \frac{37}{72}$ **(1 mark)**

12. (a) Since gradient of $CD = 1$
$\frac{3 - (m+1)}{(2m+3) - 4} = 1$ **(1 mark)**
or $2 - m = 2m - 1$
$\Rightarrow m = 1$ **(1 mark)**

(b) Coordinate of C is $(4, 2)$
So, equation of line CD is
$y = mx + c$

Or, $y = x + c$. Since $m = 1$.
Substitute $x = 4$ and $y = 2$
$2 = 4 + c, \Rightarrow c = -2$ **(1 mark)**
Hence,
$y = x - 2$ **(1 mark)**

13. (a) The next number is one of $(x-5)+5$ or $(x-5)-5$
$= x$ or $x - 10$) **(1 mark)**

(b) Let these two numbers be $x - 5$ and x
Then, based on question, $x(x - 5) = 300$

(1 mark)

$x^2 - 5x - 300 = 0$
or $(x - 20)(x + 15) = 0$ **(1 mark)**
Thus, $x = 20$ or $x = -15$
Since $x > 0$
The required numbers are
20 and $20 - 5 = 15$ **(1 mark)**

14. (a) Since we have
Use the compound growth formula
$P_T = P_0 \left(\frac{100+R}{100}\right)^T$
Substitute $R = 5$ $P_0 = 40000$.
$P_T = 40000 \left(\frac{100+5}{100}\right)^T$
$46305 = 40000 (1.05)^T$ **(1 mark)**
$(1.05)^T = \frac{46305}{40000}$
or$(1.05)^T = 1.157625$
or$(1.05)^T = (1.05)^3$
Hence, the number of years $T = 3$ years.

(1 mark)

(b) Jim is not correct.
$1.15 \times 40000 = 4600 < 46305$. **(1 mark)**

15. (a) Since the total number of students is 200,
$45 + 25 + 56 + 44 + p = 200$
$\Rightarrow p = 30$ **(1 mark)**

(b) Correct the cumulative frequency graph on the
given grid. **(2 marks)**

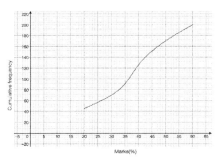

(c) The estimated pass mark from the cumulative
graph is 36%. The answers in the range of
(35% − 37%) are acceptable. **(1 mark)**

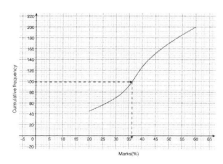

16. (a) $xy = 4200.........(i)$
$(x - 5)(y + 70) = 4200..........(ii)$ **(2 marks)**

(b) from (i) $y = \frac{4200}{x}$
So, from (ii)
$(x-5)\left(\frac{4200}{x} + 70\right) = 4200$ **(1 mark)**
$4200 + 70x - \frac{21000}{x} - 350 = 4200$
or $70x^2 - 21000 - 350x = 0$ **(1 mark)**
or, $x^2 - 5x - 300 = 0$
or $(x - 20)(x + 15) = 0$
So, $x = 20$
The number of students who went to the trip
$= x - 5$
$= 20 - 5$
$= 15$ **(1 mark)**

17. (a) $\overrightarrow{CM}$ and $\overrightarrow{MB}$ both are equal but in the opposite
sign to $\overrightarrow{BM}$ **(1 mark)**

(b) $\overrightarrow{AM} = \overrightarrow{AB} + \overrightarrow{BM}$
$\overrightarrow{AM} = \overrightarrow{AC} + \overrightarrow{CM}$ **(1 mark)**

After adding these two, we get
$2\overrightarrow{AM} = \overrightarrow{AB} + \overrightarrow{BM} + \overrightarrow{AC} + \overrightarrow{CM}$
$2\overrightarrow{AM} = \overrightarrow{AB} + \overrightarrow{AC}$ **(1 mark)**

Thus, $\overrightarrow{AM} = \frac{1}{2}\left(\overrightarrow{AB} + \overrightarrow{AC}\right)$ **(1 mark)**

18. (a) triangle AQP and triangle ABC are similar,
$\frac{QP}{CB} = \frac{AP}{AB}$ **(1 mark)**
So, $\frac{3}{x} = \frac{4}{9}$
So, $4x = 27$
$\Rightarrow x = \frac{27}{4} = 5.75\,cm$ **(1 mark)**

(b) Now, using the sine law on triangle QAP, we get
$\frac{QP}{\sin Q\hat{A}P} = \frac{AP}{\sin A\hat{Q}P}$
or $\frac{3}{\sin 45} = \frac{4}{\sin A\hat{Q}P}$
$\Rightarrow \sin A\hat{Q}P = \frac{4\sin(45)}{3}$
or $A\hat{Q}P = \sin^{-1}\left(\frac{4\sin(45)}{3}\right) = 70.528...$

(1mark)

$70.528.. + 45 + A\hat{P}Q = 180$
(Angles on the triangle AQP add up to $180°$
$\Rightarrow A\hat{P}Q = 64.471...$ **(1 mark)**
Now, the area of triangle AQP
$= \frac{1}{2}AP \times PQ \times \sin A\hat{P}Q$
$= \frac{1}{2} \times 4 \times 3 \times \sin 64.4\hat{7}1...$
$= 5.414... \approx 5.412 \mathrm{dp} cm^2$ **(1 mark)**

19. (a) $C\hat{A}D = A\hat{C}D = y$
(Base angles of the isosceles triangle ACD.) So
, $y + y = 96$
$y = 48$
(The exterior angle of the triangle is equal to the sum of the two opposite interior angles.)

(1 mark)

$A\hat{B}C = C\hat{D}E$
(The exterior angle of the cyclic quadrilateral ABCD equals the opposite interior angle.)

Thus, $A\hat{B}C = 96°$ **(1 mark)**
Now, $45 + 96 + x = 180$
$x = 39°$ **(1 mark)**

(b) $A\hat{B}C$ and $A\hat{D}C$ are supplement angles.
i.e., $A\hat{B}C + A\hat{D}C = 180°$ **(1 mark)**

20. (a) $fg(4) = f(4^2 - 2)$
$= f(14)$ **(1 mark)**
$= 3 \times 14 + 6$
$= 48$ **(1 mark)**

(b) $f(a) = 3b \rightarrow 3a + 6 = 2b$
$g(a) = b \rightarrow a^2 - 2 = b$ **(1 mark)**
So, $3a + 6 = 2(a^2 - 2)$
or $2a^2 - 3a - 10 = 0$
Solving using the formula of quadratic equation,
$a = \frac{3 \pm \sqrt{9+80}}{4}$ **(1 mark)**
Thus, $a = -1.6085... \approx -1.6(1 \text{ dp})$,
or $3.108... \approx 3.1(1 \text{ dp})$
From, $a^2 - 2 = b$
$b = 0.6 (1 \text{ dp}), 7.7 (1 \text{ dp})$ **(1 mark)**

SET B-Paper 3 Solutions

1. (a) $P(B) = \frac{3}{9} = \frac{1}{3}$.
    Now,
    $$P(\text{not } B) = 1 - \frac{1}{3} = \frac{2}{3}.$$ **(1 mark)**

    (b) No, Tom is not correct.
    When taking 4 elements of A and 3 elements of B, common element 2 repeats in both sets and, hence, is counted twice.
    The correct solution is
    $$P(A \cup B) = \frac{4}{9} + \frac{3}{9} - \frac{1}{9} = \frac{6}{9} = \frac{2}{3}.$$ **(1 mark)**

2. (a) Percentage of health $= \frac{1}{4}$ of $100\% = 25\%$ **(1 mark)**

    Percentage of education
    $$= \frac{72}{360} \times 100\% = 20\%$$ **(1 mark)**

    (b) Let the expense of the 'other' title be $x\%$.
    Then,
    $20 + 20 + 25 + x = 100$
    $\Rightarrow x = 35$ **(1 mark)**
    So, $35\% = 525$
    $\Rightarrow 1\% = \frac{525}{35}$
    $\Rightarrow 100\% = \frac{525}{35} \times 100 = \$1500$ **(1 mark)**

3. (a) A 100 g jar costs £1.5.
    1 g costs $\frac{1.5}{100} = £0.015$ **(1 mark)**
    A 200 g jar costs £2.5.
    1 g costs $\frac{2.5}{200} = £0.0125$ **(1 mark)**
    A 450 g jar costs £5.
    1 g costs $\frac{5}{450} = £0.0\dot{1}$
    Therefore, £5 for 450 g is least costly. **(1 mark)**

    (b) Since the 450 g jar is the least costly, Harry has to buy the maximum number of 450 g jar. He buys two 200 g jars and three 450 g jars of honey.
    (1 mark)

    Hence, the total cost is
    $= £2 \times 5 + 3 \times 2.5 = £17.5$
    (2 marks)

4. (a) The ratio of X and Y is $3:4$.
    And the ratio of Y and Z is $2:3$.
    Let's make the Y part equal in both ratios.
    The ratio of Y and Z can be written as $4:6$.
    Now, the ratio of X, Y and Z is $3:4:6$.
    The total parts are $6 + 4 + 3 = 13$
    (1 mark)
    The difference between the X and Z parts is 3.

Therefore, 3 parts $= £12 \Rightarrow 1$ part $= £4$
Hence, the total for 13 parts $= 4 \times 13$
$= £52$.
(1 mark)

An alternative solution of (a):
Since, X : Y = 3 : 4 and Y : Z = 2 : 3 = 4 : 6, we can write X: Y: Z = 3: 4: 6.
The total parts = $6 + 4 + 3 = 13$.
(1 mark)
The difference between the X and Z parts is 3.
Therefore, 3 parts $= £12 \Rightarrow 1$ part $= £4$
Hence, a total of 13 parts $= 4 \times 13$
$= £52$.
(1 mark)

(b) Amount for $X = 3 \times 4 = £12$
Amount for $Y = 4 \times 4 = £16$
Amount for $Z = 6 \times 4 = £24$
(2 marks)

5. (a)

	Head (H)	Tail (T)
1	(1, H)	(1,T)
2	(2,H)	(2,T)
3	(3,H)	(3,T)
4	(4,H)	(4,T)
5	(5,H)	(5,T)
6	(6,H)	(6,T)

(2 marks)

(b) The probability of heads and an even number
$= \frac{3}{12} = \frac{1}{4}$.
(1 mark)

6. Each interior angle on a pentagon is $= \frac{180 \times (5-2)}{5} = 108°$
    Each angle of the square is $90°$.
    The angles on a point H add up to $360°$ So,
    $A\hat{H}G + A\hat{H}C + C\hat{H}G = 360° \Rightarrow x + 90° + 108° = 360°$
    (1 mark)
    $\Rightarrow x = 360° - 198° = 162°$
    (1 mark)
    Also, $B\hat{C}D + D\hat{C}E + E\hat{C}H + B\hat{C}H = 360°$

$$y + 60° + 108° + 90° = 360°$$
$$\Rightarrow y = 360° - 258°$$
$$= 102° \qquad \textbf{(1 mark)}$$

7. (a) Number of bacteria after 3 days
$$= P_0(1 + r)^t \qquad \textbf{(1 mark)}$$
$$= 2.3 \times 10^8 (1 - \tfrac{10}{100})^3$$
$$= 1.67 \times 10^8 \qquad \textbf{(2 marks)}$$

(b) Yes. The rate of decrease in the number of bacteria is $P_0(0.9)^t$. This value is always greater than zero for any large value of t. **(1 mark)**

8. (a) Accelerration $(a) = \frac{v-u}{t} = \frac{100-40}{4}$
$$= 15 m/s^2. \qquad \textbf{(2 marks)}$$

(b) Rekha is not correct. Since acceleration is the rate of change on velocity, a constant velocity gives zero acceleration. **(1 mark)**

(c) The distance from A to D is the area below ABCD and above x-axis $= 4 \times 40 + \frac{1}{2} \times 4 \times 60 + 6 \times 100 + \frac{1}{2}4 \times 100$
$$= 160 + 120 + 600 + 200 \qquad \textbf{(2 marks)}$$
$$= 1080\, m \qquad \textbf{(1 mark)}$$

9. Here, radius $(r) = 14\, cm$
Therefore, the lower limit of $r = 13.5\, cm$
The upper limit of $r = 14.5\, cm$ **(1 mark)**
And area $A = 616\, cm^2$
The lower limit of $A = 615.5\, cm^2$
The upper limit of $A = 616.5\, cm^2$ **(1 mark)**
Now, the upper bound for the value of $\pi =$
$$\frac{\text{Upper limit of A}}{(\text{Lower limit of r})^2}$$
$$= \frac{616.5}{13.5^2} = 3.38\,(3 \text{ s.f.}). \qquad \textbf{(1 mark)}$$
The lower bound for the value of $\pi = \frac{\text{Lower limit of A}}{(\text{Upper limit of r})^2}$
$$= \frac{615.5}{14.5^2} = 2.93\,(3 \text{ s.f.}). \qquad \textbf{(1 mark)}$$

10. (a) Here,
the length of the pendulum $= r = 40\, cm$
The length of arc $= l = 60\, cm$

$$\frac{\theta}{360} \times \pi \times 2 \times 40 = 60$$
(1 mark)

$$\frac{\theta}{360^9} \times \pi \times 2 \times \cancel{40} = \frac{2\pi\theta}{9} = 60$$

$$2\pi\theta = 9 \times 60$$

$$\theta = \frac{540}{2\pi} = \frac{270}{\pi}$$
(1 mark)

(b) Now,
Area of sector $= \frac{\theta}{360} \times \pi \times r^2$
$$= \frac{85.94}{360} \times \pi \times 40^2$$
$$= 1200\, cm^2. \qquad \textbf{(2 marks)}$$

11.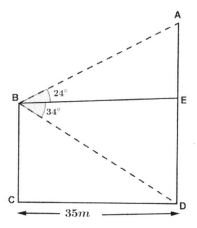

From the figure, AC is height of building A, and BD is the height of building B.
$$B\hat{D}C = E\hat{B}D = 34°$$
From $\triangle BCD, \tan B\hat{D}C = \frac{BC}{CD} \Rightarrow \tan 34° = \frac{BC}{35.}$
Therefore, the height of building $A = BC = 23.6\, m$
(1 mark)

Again $BE = CD = 35\, m$
From $\triangle ABE, \tan A\hat{B}E = \frac{AE}{BE}$
$$\Rightarrow \tan 24 = \frac{AE}{35} \Rightarrow AE = 15.58\, m$$
Therefore, the height of building B $= AD$
$= 23.6 + 15.58 = 39.18 \approx: 39.2\, m\,(2 \text{ d.p.})$ **(2 marks)**

12. (a) $43 + 15 = 58$ and $58 + 17 = 75$
Therefore, the two numbers in the sequence are 58 and 75. **(1 mark)**

(b) The second difference is 2 (a constant).
Therefore, this sequence is quadratic.
It has the nth term of the form $an^2 + bn + c$.
The second difference is 2. Therefore,
$$2a = 2 \Rightarrow a = 1 \qquad \textbf{(1 mark)}$$
The first term of the sequence is 3.
So, substitute $n = 1$ to give
$a(1)^2 + b(1) + c = 3,$
$2 + b + c = 3$
or,
$b + c = 1...(i)$.
The second term of the sequence is 10.
So, when $n = 2$, we get,
$a(2)^2 + b(2) + c = 10$
$2(2^2) + 2b + c = 10$
$2b + c = 2...(ii)$
Subtracting equation (i) from (ii) gives $b = 1$
(1 mark)
Substituting the value of b in (ii) gives $c = -2$

Therefore, nth term of the sequence is n^2+4n-2.
(**1 mark**)

(c) For 10th term, let $n = 10$ on $n^2 + 4n - 2$
Then $10^2 + 4 \times 10 - 2$
$= 138$. (**1 mark**)

13. The height, l of the square-based pyramid is $11 - 6 = 5\, cm$.
The base, b of the triangle is $8\, cm$.
Then the height, h of the triangle is given by
$h^2 = l^2 + (\frac{b}{2})^2 = 5^2 + (\frac{8}{2})^2$
$\Rightarrow h = \sqrt{5^2 + 4^2} = 6.4\, m$ (**1 mark**)
The total surface area of the shape
$=$ Area of the four triangles $+$ Area of the four rectangles
$= 4 \times \frac{1}{2} \times 6.4 \times 8 + 4 \times 8 \times 6$
$= 294.4\, m^2$ (**2 marks**)

Now the total cost $= 294.4 \times 2.15$
$= £632.96$. (**1 mark**)

14. Here, $y - 2 = \sqrt{\frac{x+4}{x-m}}$.
Squaring both sides $y^2 - 4y + 4 = \frac{x+4}{x-m}$ (**1 mark**)
$(x - m)(y^2 - 4y + 4) = x + 4$
$xy^2 - 4xy + 4x - y^2m + 4ym - 4m = x + 4$
$\Rightarrow xy^2 - 4xy + 4x - x = my^2 - 4my + 4m + y$
$\Rightarrow x(y^2 - 4y + 3) = my^2 - 4my + 4m + 4$
$\Rightarrow x = \frac{my^2 - 4my + 4m + 4}{y^2 - 4y + 3}$ (**2 marks**)

15. (a) Consider $x^2 - x - 20 = 0$
$\Rightarrow (x - 5)(x + 4) = 0$
Therefore, $x = 5$, or -4. (**1 mark**)
For $6 > 5$ and $-5 < -4$ inequality is not true.
Therefore, the solution is
$-4 <\le x \le 5$. (**1 mark**)

(b) And solution on number line is

(**1mark**)

16. Let Naved's age be x, and his younger brother's age be y.
Then,
$x + y = 17. \ldots \ldots \ldots (i)$
$x^2 + y^2 = 149. \ldots \ldots (ii)$
From (i) $x = 17 - y$

Substituting value of x on (ii)
$(17 - y)^2 + y^2 = 149$ $289 - 34y + y^2 + y^2 = 149$
$2y^2 - 34y + 140 = 0$
$y^2 - 17y + 70 = 0$
$(y - 9(y - 10) = 0$
$y = 7$ or $y = 10$ (**2 marks**)
We substitute the value of y in (i) to get
$x = 7, 10$
Therefore, Naved's age is ten years and his younger brother's age is seven years. (**2 marks**)

17. (a) For $x = 0$, $x^3 - 5x - 4 = -4 < 0$
For $x = 3$, $x^3 - 5x - 4 = 8 > 0$
The function is continuous in the given interval and sign changes occur.
Therefore, there lies a root between 0 and 3.
(**1 mark**)

(b) Here, $x^3 - 5x - 4 = 0$
or, $x^3 = 5x + 4$
or, $x^2 = 5 + \frac{4}{x}$
Therefore, $x = \sqrt{5 + \frac{4}{x}}$ (**2 marks**)

(c) For $x_0 = 1$, $x_1 = \sqrt{5 + \frac{4}{1}} = 3$
For $x_1 = 3$, $x_2 = \sqrt{5 + \frac{4}{3}}$
$= 2.5166... \approx 2.52 (2.5\, d.p.)$ (**1 mark**)
For $x_2 = 2.5166..$, $x_3 = \sqrt{5 + \frac{4}{2.5166...}}$
$= 2.56699... \approx 2.57 (2\, d.p.)$. (**1 mark**)
For $x_3 = 2.5609... \approx 2.56 (2\, d.p.)$,
$x_4 = \sqrt{5 + \frac{4}{2.5609...}} = 2.5616... \approx 2.562\, d.p.)$.
Therefore, the required solution is $x = 2.56$.
(**1 mark**)

18. of $y = 2f(x)$ is

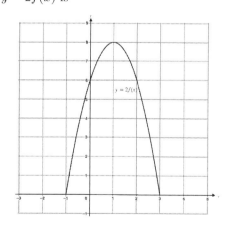

(**3 marks**)
$y = -f(x)$ is symmetric about the line $x = 1$.
(**1 mark**)

(19)   (a)

$0 < n \le 15$	4
$15 < n \le 30$	2
$30 < n \le 40$	5
$40 < n \le 60$	11
$60 < n \le 70$	3
$70 < n \le 85$	4
$85 < n \le 95$	3
$95 < n \le 100$	2

(3 marks)

(b) The total frequency is 49.

Median is $\frac{49}{2} = 24.5^{th}$ value.

This lies on the interval $40 < n \le 60$.

$6 + 3 + 5 = 14$

So $\frac{24.5 - 14}{36 - 14} = \frac{10.5}{22}$ of $(60 - 40) = 9\frac{6}{11}\%$ **(1 mark)**

Hence the median score is $40 + 9\frac{6}{11} = 49\frac{6}{11} \approx$ 49.5%   **(1 mark)**

(c) There are 5 students who get marks between 30% and 40%.

The number of people who scored between 30% and 40% is

$0.5 \times 4 = 2$ **(1 mark)**

Hence, the total number of students who failed the test is $2 + 3 + 4 + 6 = 11$

Therefore, total student who passed the test

$= 49 - 11 = 38$ **(1 mark)**

Printed in Great Britain
by Amazon

80112359R00099